RUG WEAVING
technique and design

Brian Knight

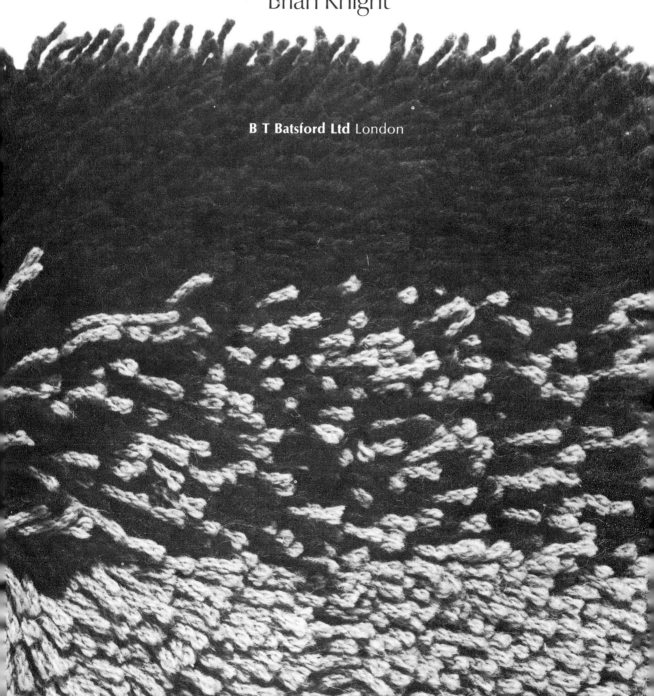

B T Batsford Ltd London

Acknowledgment

I would like to thank all those friends and colleagues who over the years and in a variety of ways have encouraged and assisted me in the writing of this book.

My special thanks go to Marienne Straub and to John O'Connor without whom it would never have begun; to Peter Collingwood who very kindly provided the photographs of his work and thus helped bring the work to a speedier conclusion; to Frank Thurston of the Royal College of Art who can always be relied upon to do a perfect job and whose beautiful photographs illustrate the woven samples.

Finally I would like to thank John Tovey to whom I am much indebted. His technical knowledge and experience have succeeded in making the book technically accurate and as general reader he has given a great deal of his valuable time. His contribution in writing the sections on the countermarch loom, and calculating quantities is much appreciated.

First published 1980
© Brian Knight 1980

ISBN 0 7134 2582 2

Printed in Great Britain by
The Anchor Press, Tiptree, Essex
for the publishers B T Batsford Ltd,
4 Fitzhardinge Street, London W1H 0AH

CONTENTS

PREFACE

For the many people who are interested in weaving their own rugs, but are daunted by the prospect of studying technique and design, the following pages describe and illustrate simply and clearly the basic rug weaving techniques, so that the beginner may be able to tackle the craft with confidence.

It is to be emphasised that however simple a technique may be, it is only by the practical experience of weaving and the use of the imagination, that ideas for designs are conceived.

One of the results of designing in this way is to discover that so often the most practical way of using a technique leads to a type of design with a strongly traditional flavour.

The most practical way for a beginner to start, is to experiment with samples of about 300 mm (12 in.) square. These provide a reasonable area on which to work, while at the same time making unpicking and re-weaving much less irksome and time-consuming. One of the most important considerations when designing a rug is the choice of technique. In this book the most simple rug weaving techniques are described, almost all of them based on plain weave. At the same time a wide range of types of design is explored, with explanations of methods used to create different effects.

The other important decision is the choice of colour. This can be influenced by a number of factors, such as the place for which the rug is required, a liking for a particular colour, or for natural colours. The examples in this book encourage the reader to use related colours based on one particular hue. In chapter 12 on Soumak, for example, the colours of magenta, orange/brown, carmine, deep madder and scarlet are based upon the idea of red. In chapter 13 on warp-faced weaves, the colour chosen is blue, and in chapter 11 on Khelim, yellow.

Unless it is the intention to weave matting or rag rugs, there is virtually no choice in the type of material used, as most rugs are woven in wool, though care must be taken to ensure that the weight of yarn, tightness of spin and the kind of fleece used are all suitable for the rug being designed.

The suggested range of equipment has been reduced to a

minimum. Often simple, home-made devices are as efficient and as easy to use as the commercial alternatives. The items discussed in chapter 1 are all that are absolutely necessary. Throughout the book, the metric and imperial sizes given are not necessarily the exact equivalents of each other, but are comparable standard sizes in the two systems. It is important to keep to one system of measurement and not to mix them.

1 BASIC WEAVING EQUIPMENT

Warp and weft

Woven material, if closely observed, will be seen to be made up of two sets of interlaced threads, these are known as the *warp* and the *weft*. The warp is the set of threads running vertically through the weaving, and upon which the fabric is constructed. The word 'warp' is derived from the fact that these threads are 'warped' or stretched during weaving.

The weft threads lie at right angles to the warp. They are carried by the shuttle and interlace with the warp threads, forming the width of the cloth. Figure 1.1 shows the warp and weft weaving in its simplest form — plain weave.

During the actual process of weaving, the warp threads are held at an even tension and at the correct spacing on either a frame or a loom.

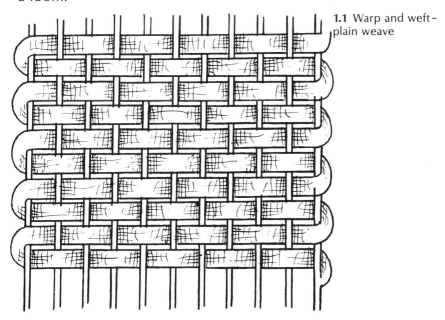

1.1 Warp and weft – plain weave

Warp yarns

Warp yarns, because of the tension placed upon them, need to be generally harder, finer and more tightly spun than those in the weft. Cotton and linen are the two fibres most often used for this purpose. Cotton netting twine is strongly recommended for beginners, as its elasticity helps considerably in achieving an even tension in the warp. Linen makes an excellent warp, but is entirely without elasticity, and is difficult to tension without experience.

Wool also makes an excellent warp if tightly spun, and so do goat- and camel-hair. All these yarns are available from suppliers, and have the elasticity which makes them suitable for use by beginners.

Weft yarns

Wool yarns for rug weaving are most frequently used in three weights – 2, 3 and 6-ply. The weft yarns can be softer, thicker and less regular than the warp yarns.

Many weavers, given sufficient time, prefer to spin their own yarns if they need special characteristics unobtainable in the usual commercially-available yarns. Commercial yarns can be plied together to obtain different textures or qualities.

Other natural and man-made fibres and materials can be used, including coir, sisal, rush, sea-grass, rag, strips of knitted nylon and even metallic yarns and strip cellophane. These materials, however, are best used in association with one another and *not* mixed with wool.

The most important items of equipment needed in rug weaving are described below. Only those marked with an asterisk are absolutely essential for a beginner.

Shuttles*

The two types of shuttles most suitable for rug weaving are the ski-shuttle and the stick shuttle.

The ski-shuttle
The ski-shuttle, figure 1.2(a) and (b), is ideally suited to the horizontal loom, as it will slide easily through the shed, making weaving across a wide warp much less tiring. The weft yarn is wound round the wooden hooks in a circular path, figure 1.2(b).

The stick shuttle
The stick shuttle, figure 1.3, is, by contrast, at its most useful on a vertical warp, where the weft yarn is required to be passed from hand to hand. Stick shuttles vary in length from 1 m (39 in.) down to 250 mm (10 in.), the shorter ones being invaluable for weaving small samples. Yarns are wound onto stick shuttles as shown in figure 1.3, a slip knot is tied in the end of the yarn and placed on the peg. The yarn is then taken down, round the base and up the other side and once more over the peg. This is continued until the required length of yarn has been wound. See also page 55.

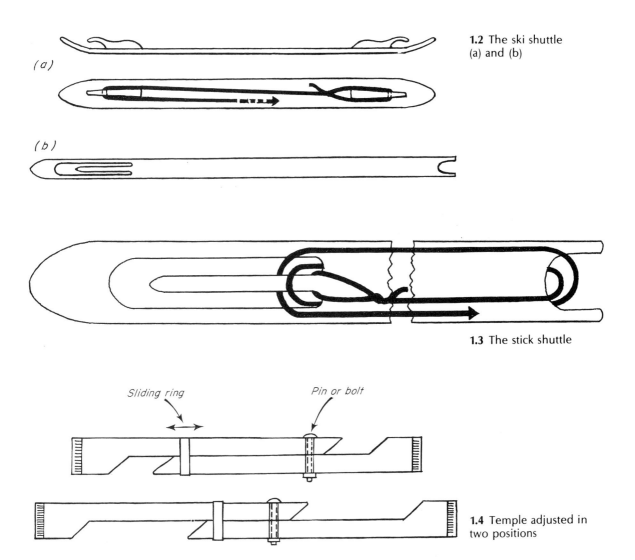

1.2 The ski shuttle (a) and (b)

(a)

(b)

1.3 The stick shuttle

Sliding ring   Pin or bolt

1.4 Temple adjusted in two positions

Temple or tenterhook figure 1.4

A temple or tenterhook is a useful item of equipment when weaving weft-faced rugs. It is used to hold out the fabric to its full width whilst in the process of weaving, to ensure that the edges remain straight. It is constructed of two wooden bars which are hinged together and can be adjusted in length to match the width of the weaving by means of a pin or small bolt near the centre. Each end is bevelled and has a row of sharp metal teeth set in at an angle. The temple is unlocked by sliding the ring away from the pin and along its own side until it clears the free end of the other half, and then set to the correct length. The teeth are inserted into the edges of the rug with the temple partially folded into an inverted 'V', and then pressed down onto the cloth, stretching it out in the process, and locked into position by sliding the ring

11

back onto the end of the free half. The temple is not an essential piece of equipment, but it does make it much easier to keep the weaving out to the full width and prevent 'waisting', figure 1.5.

1.5 Waisted weaving

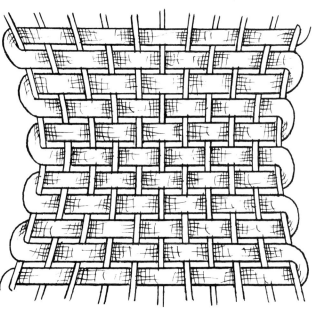

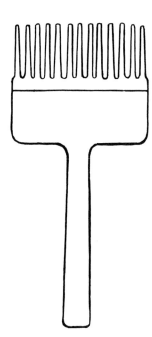

1.6 Hand beater

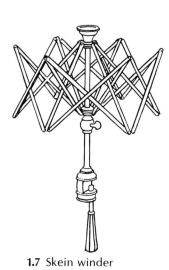

1.7 Skein winder

Forks and hand beaters

Hand beaters are most frequently employed on upright looms and rug frames when a particularly close weave is required. They are also useful when employing the Khelim and the Tapestry techniques, when the work builds up on several different levels during the course of weaving the pattern and a batten cannot be used. More pressure can be applied with the beater than with the fingers, when the weaving demands it. Of the types available metal beaters are the most efficient, though old table forks can be used. The prongs do not need to have the same spacing as the warp threads.

Skein winder

The skein winder or swift is a useful piece of equipment, as most yarns are sold in hanks. Various types of swift are available. The umbrella type from Scandinavia, figure 1.7, works well and is easily adjusted. It can be set up to work either horizontally or vertically. Another type is the floor rice, which has two revolving circular cages with flanged ends to hold the yarn.

Raddle*

The purpose of the raddle is to spread the warp threads evenly to the required width across the loom before they are rolled onto the

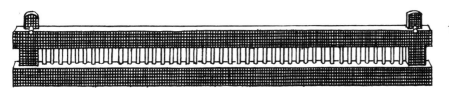

1.8 Raddle

warp beam, figure 1.8. The cap or top bar of the raddle is removable to facilitate threading, and is replaced to hold the warp threads in position whilst winding on.

Warping mill or frame*

The warping mill and the warping board, figures 1.9 and 1.10, are both for winding a comparatively large number of threads which have all to be of the same length and at the same tension. On a mill, the threads are wound in a spiral between the upper and lower sets of pegs, and on a board or frame they zigzag from side to side. Both pieces of apparatus are equally efficient, but while the mill is quicker to use it is also more expensive and occupies more space when it is not being used. A warping board is easily made from a piece of blockboard or heavy plywood, with pegs of dowelling 25 mm - 40 mm (1 in. - 1½ in.), or of broom handle. (Figure 1.11 is a dimensioned working drawing of a board.)

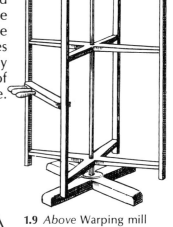

1.9 *Above* Warping mill

1.10 *Left* Warping board

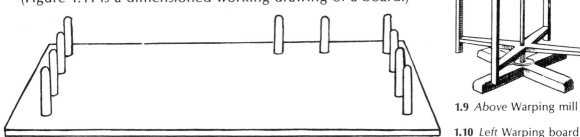

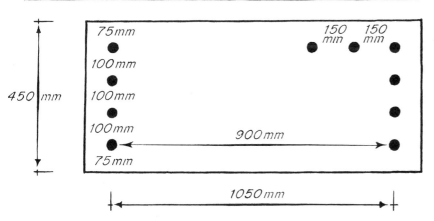

1.11 Dimensioned working drawing of a warping board

Spool rack

A spool rack, figure 1.12, is a wooden frame which carries a number of iron rods of approximately 6 mm (¼ in.) diameter upon

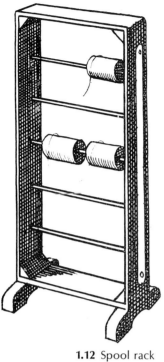

1.12 Spool rack

which the spools of yarn can be placed. A cheap and reasonably efficient substitute is a spool stand or cop rack, which is a small board with vertical pegs to hold the spools or cops of yarn, figure 1.13. The best board is made with pegs of 12 mm (½ in.) dowelling about 150 mm - 200 mm (6 in. - 8 in.) long and pressed into holes in the board, but a simple alternative is to hammer some 150 mm (6 in.) nails through a piece of hardboard.

Cross-sticks* figure 1.14

These are slightly rounded wooden sticks, the width of the loom in length, and used to separate the warp threads and to hold the cross (figure 1.15). There is a hole bored at each end through which twine can be tied to prevent them from slipping out of the warp.

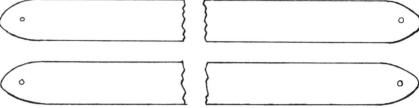

1.14 Cross sticks

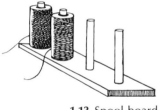

1.13 Spool board

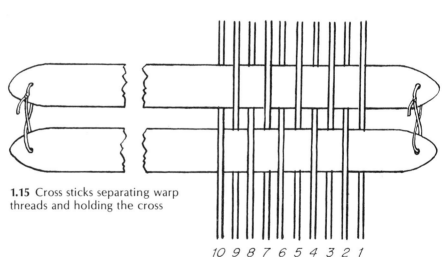

1.15 Cross sticks separating warp threads and holding the cross

10 9 8 7 6 5 4 3 2 1

Threading hook*

This is a long, flat strip of metal with a hook cut in one end and a short wooden handle on the other. It is used for entering warp threads through the eyes of the heddles, figure 1.16.

1.16 Threading hook

Reed hook

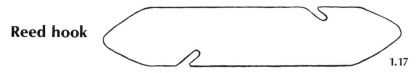

1.17

A flat double-ended hook, thin enough to pass through the dents in the reed (ie the spaces between the reed wires). Used for drawing the threads through the reed, figure 1.17.

Scissors*

Textile scissors or weaver's snips are designed to be held in the palm of the hand, figure 1.18, to keep the working fingers free.

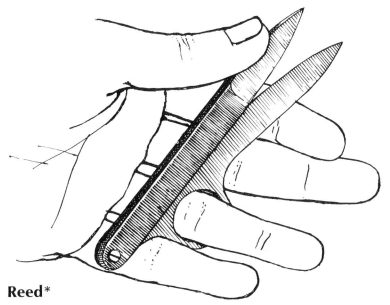

1.18 Textile scissors

Reed*

The reed, figure 1.19, is used to space out the warp threads, and beat-up the weft threads. It forms a guide for the shuttle. It is made of thin, vertical strips of metal (reed wires) set in strong rods (baulks) at the top and bottom. The number of spaces or dents to 10 cm (metric) or to 1 in. (imperial) is the sett of the reed. The most useful setts for rug weaving are 16 and 24 to 10 cm (4 and 6 to 1 in.).

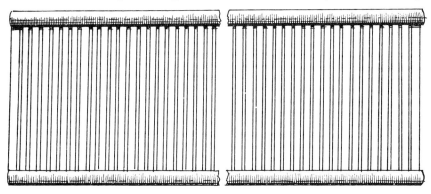

1.19 The reed

2 THE WEAVING FRAME

Home made wooden frames are easy to build and can be any size. Those described here are suitable for beginners who have not previously constructed a weaving frame and are uncertain what type to use.

There are basically two types of weaving frame, which differ in the method of attaching the warp to the frame.

Type 1 Fixed warp
The warp is fastened directly to the frame, which restricts the weaving length to approximately two-thirds of the length of the frame.

Type 2 Tensioned warp
The warp is placed on two rods and then wrapped round the frame, tension being obtained by drawing the rods together by means of a strong lacing cord. Small frames can be used by the weaver while sitting at a table, but larger frames capable of accommodating full-sized rugs have to be secured firmly to a wall or other support before use.

Frame 1 Fixed warp

This is a convenient size for weaving design samples and for practice, and takes a 300 mm (12 in.) warp, figure 2.1.

Timber requirements
Planed white timber (pine) is recommended as it is light, easily cut and is unlikely to split when nails and screws are used.

Four pieces of timber are required*
2 lengths A and B 25 mm x 50 mm x 750 mm (1 in. x 2 in. x 30 in.)
2 lengths C and D 12 mm x 50 mm x 500 mm (½ in. x 2 in. x 20 in.)

Construction
The two side pieces A and B are placed 400 mm (26 in.) apart and the frame completed by placing lengths C and D on top of them at the four corners. The corners should be checked with a set square

*NB The metric and imperial measurements are not exact equivalents, but are convenient sizes in each system. Do *not* mix the systems.

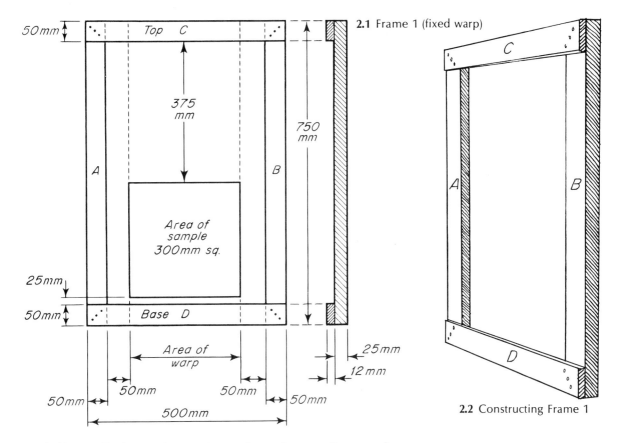

50mm

Top C

375 mm

750 mm

A

B

Area of sample 300mm sq.

25mm

50mm   Base D

Area of warp

50mm   50mm

50mm ←→   50mm ←→ 50mm

500mm

25mm

12mm

2.1 Frame 1 (fixed warp)

C

A   B

D

2.2 Constructing Frame 1

and then nailed together, using at least three nails at each corner. If no set square is available, the accuracy can be checked by ensuring that the two diagonals of the frame are equal, figure 2.2.

Threading up the frame
First mark the centres of the top and bottom bars of the frame, and then mark off at 10 mm (½ in.) intervals for 150 mm (6 in.). This will ensure that the weaving is placed centrally in the frame.

The warp is now wound firmly round the frame at 5 mm (¼ in.) intervals, using the marks to ensure accuracy. Cotton is recommended for samples, as it is strong and elastic. A medium fine yarn should be used. On a large frame, to keep the strain evenly balanced, the warp should be started in the centre and wound outwards in two halves. On a small frame such as the one described, the warp can be wound from one side to the other.

Warping is started by tying the end of the yarn onto the left hand end of the top bar, over the first mark. The thread is taken down the back of the frame, round underneath, and up the front, as tightly as possible. The first finger of the left hand is placed on the yarn where it crosses the top of the frame to maintain the tension whilst the next thread is being wound on, figure 2.3. Double the first and last threads to make a firm selvedge.

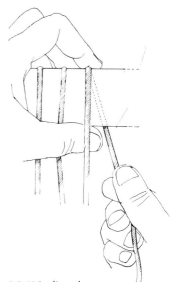

2.3 Winding the warp

An evenly tensioned warp is essential for successful weaving. Feel the surface of the warp with the tips of the fingers to check the evenness of the tension. If it is not even, start at one side of the warp and pull each thread to the front of the frame, keeping the first finger on each thread in turn as it is tightened, so that the tension does not slip back. When the other side is reached, untie the end to dispose of the slack, and re-tie as before.

The shed

In plain weave, the weft threads go under and over the threads of the warp one at a time. The quickest way to do this is to raise all the threads under which the shuttle must pass, and leave the others down, to make a small triangular tunnel through which the shuttle can pass. This tunnel is called the *shed*, and in plain weave there are just two sheds, the odd numbered warp threads up for the first, and the even ones up for the second. In this first weaving frame, one shed is created by the top bar of the loom itself, one set of threads being held permanently in front of the other. For the second shed, the order of threads must be reversed, the back ones being brought forward about 25 mm (1 in.) in front of the front threads, so that the shuttle can pass under them. For this operation, twine loops called *leashes* are fastened round the back threads.

Tying the leashes

Leashes are made on the loom by cutting lengths of cotton twine about 375 mm (15 in.) long, looping one round each back warp thread, bringing the ends out between the pair of warp threads in the front layer on either side of it and then tying the ends of each leash together, leaving about 25 mm (1 in.) beyond the knot, figure 2.4. When all the leashes have been made, they are tied together in bunches of six, figure 2.5, and pushed up to the top of the frame.

To start weaving, bring the first bunch of leashes at one edge down to the centre of the warp, and then pull it upwards towards you, to bring the back threads up in front of the front threads. Pass the shuttle through this shed, figure 2.6, and return the bunch of leashes to the top of the loom. Repeat this sequence with each bunch in turn right across the loom. The weft must lie in an arc from side to side of the loom before it is beaten down, as it has to bend round the warp threads when it is in place, and if enough slack is not left at this stage, the weaving will be pulled in at the sides. The thread should be pressed down in several places with the fingers to distribute the slack evenly across the width of the weaving before it is finally beaten down into place with a metal hand beater, figure 2.7. The return row is straightforward, as the return shed is formed permanently by the top bar of the frame.

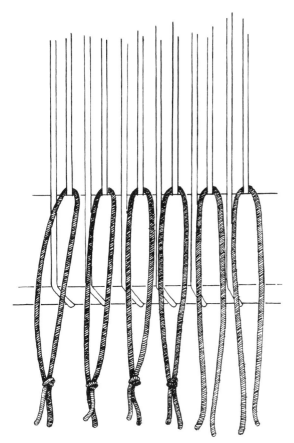

2.4 Tying the leashes

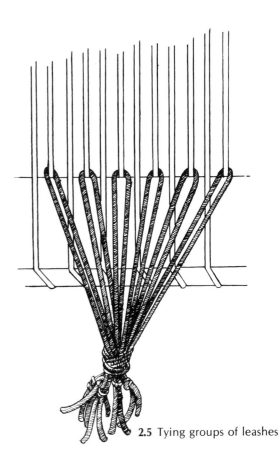

2.5 Tying groups of leashes

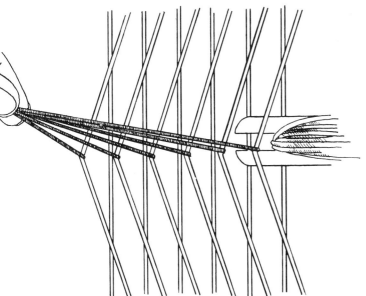

2.6 Second shed by pulling up leashes

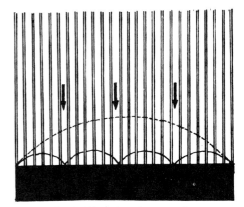

2.7 Method of beating down weft yarn

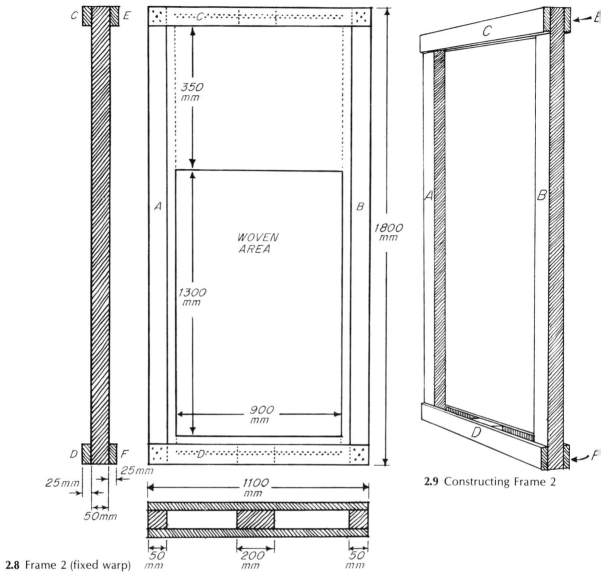

2.8 Frame 2 (fixed warp)

2.9 Constructing Frame 2

Frame 2 Fixed warp (medium to large frame) *figure 2.8*

Timber requirements
Six pieces of timber are required*
2 lengths A and B 50 mm x 50 mm x 1800 mm (2 in. x 2 in. x 72 in.)
4 lengths C, D, E, F 25 mm x 50 mm x 1100 mm (1 in. x 2 in. x 40 in.)
and also
2 lengths 50 mm x 50 mm x 200 mm (2 in. x 2 in. x 8 in.)
2 lengths 25 mm x 5 mm x 900 mm (1 in. x $\frac{3}{16}$ in. x 36 in.)
1 length of dowelling 20 mm x 900 mm ($\frac{3}{4}$ in. x 36 in.)

*NB   The metric and imperial measurements are not exact equivalents, but are convenient sizes in each system. Do *not* mix the systems.

Construction

As with frame 1, the top and bottom pieces C and D are placed on top of the two side pieces A and B. In addition to these, two more pieces E and F are placed at the back of the side pieces to strengthen the frame in the larger version. Nail the corners together, working from the outside of the timber, using five 50 mm (2 in.) nails at each corner. Additional blocks of wood, about 50 mm x 50 mm x 200 mm (2 in. x 2 in. x 8 in.) should be nailed centrally between the two top and the two bottom bars. This frame will take a rug up to 900 mm x 1300 mm (36 in. x 50 in.), figure 2.9.

Threading up the frame

The warp threads on this frame do not go round the top and bottom bars as in frame 1, but are wound up and down between two rows of nails driven in at an angle into the bars of the loom, figure 2.10. As on frame 1, marks are made at 10 mm (½ in.) intervals along the top and bottom bars, starting at the centre and working outwards. To prevent the wood from splitting, the rows of nails must be staggered by about 25 mm (1 in.). The warp threads can be arranged in a number of different ways to give different setts to 100 mm (1 in.). Figures 2.11 and 2.12 show the arrangements of yarn and nails for 16 ends per 100 mm (4 ends per inch) and 24 ends per 100 mm (6 ends per inch) respectively.

On a frame of this size the warp is wound on in two halves, starting at the centre and working to the edges. First secure the frame firmly to the wall or other support. Make a knot, figure 2.13, in the end of the warp yarn and pass it round the central nail in the top bar. Bring the thread down, pass it round the central nail in the bottom bar and continue to pass round each nail in turn at the top and bottom alternately until the half of the warp is complete. Make the selvedge thread double for extra strength, and twist the thread round the final nail to retain the tension before tying the final knot. Repeat this whole process for the second half, starting again from the centre nail (figure 2.14).

The tension must be checked when the warping is finished, by running the tips of the fingers across the warp from side to side, and if it is not perfectly even the threads must be re-tensioned, starting from the centre once more and working outwards, as described for frame 1. When the tension is correct, the last knot is untied and re-tied at the new tension. Warping round nails instead of round the end bars of the loom brings all the threads to the same level instead of being in two separate layers, so that the next operation is to create the first shed.

The shed stick

The shed stick is a smooth, flat length of wood with rounded edges, about 25 mm to 35 mm (1 in. to 1½ in.) wide and 4 mm to 5 mm (³⁄₁₆ in.) thick. The length will depend on the width of the

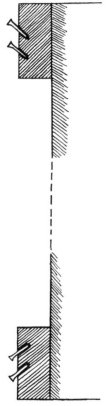

2.10 Nails for warp set at an angle

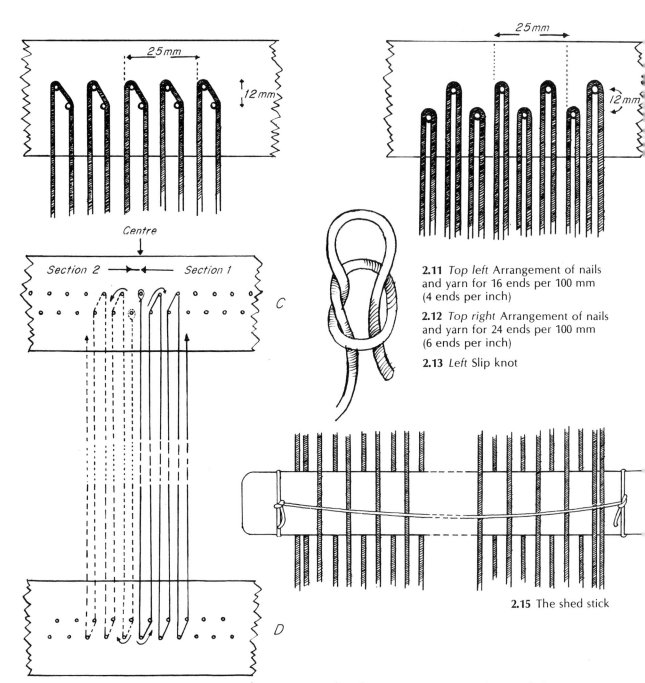

2.11 *Top left* Arrangement of nails and yarn for 16 ends per 100 mm (4 ends per inch)

2.12 *Top right* Arrangement of nails and yarn for 24 ends per 100 mm (6 ends per inch)

2.13 *Left* Slip knot

2.15 The shed stick

2.14 *Above* Threading up Frame 2 (warp in two sections)

warp and must extend at least 50 mm (2 in.) beyond the warp at each side. For this frame the stick will be 1.2 m (3 ft 4 in.) long. To make the first shed, the stick must be woven into the warp under and over alternate threads as in figure 2.15, remembering the double threads for the selvedge at each side. Tie a piece of thread from the top end of the stick right across the warp, to prevent the stick from slipping out of the shed. To open the shed, turn the stick on edge.

Tying the leashes

For the second shed, leashes are needed, and are made as before by tying lengths of twine round the set of warp threads that are under the shed stick. On the larger frame the leashes are tied to a rod, to facilitate the raising of the leashes.

Tying the leashes to a rod can be done in one of two ways; (i) by tying the leashes individually, or (ii) by knotting loops at regular intervals in a length of thread and then picking up the loops, round the warp threads and onto a leash rod, one by one across the width of the warp.

Tying leashes individually

2.16 G-clamp size 4

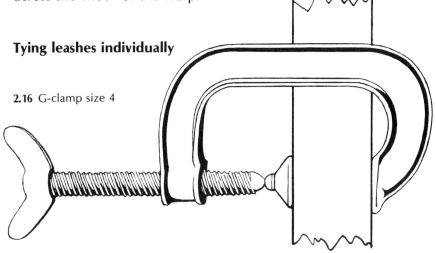

Position a G-clamp (size 4), figure 2.16, half way up the frame on each side so that the screws are projecting towards you, and tie the dowelling rod firmly to them at each end with string, figure 2.17.

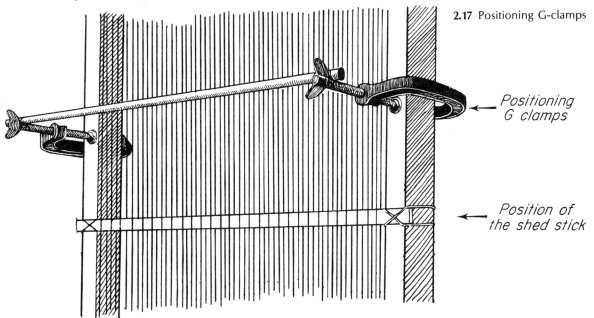

2.17 Positioning G-clamps

← Positioning G clamps

← Position of the shed stick

23

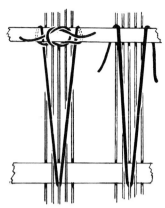

2.18 Tying leashes

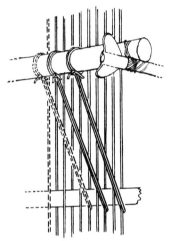

2.19 Tying leashes – comprehensive view

Cut cotton twine into lengths of about 600 mm (24 in.) for the leashes. Position the shed stick about 250 mm (10 in.) below the line of the dowelling and tie firmly at either side of the frame to keep it in position. A pre-cut length of twine is now passed behind one of the lower set of warp threads, at a point below the shed stick, and the ends are brought up to the dowelling, figure 2.18(a), to be knotted round it with a reef knot, figure 2.18(b). To ensure that the leashes are all the same length, they should all be at the same tension, (just taut), when they are tied between the shed stick and the dowelling, figure 2.19. When all the leashes have been tied, cut the strings holding the shed stick, and position it at the top of the frame. This method of tying the leashes has the advantage that the leashes are held in position ready for use all the time, and are easily drawn forward in groups with one hand while the shuttle is passed behind the raised warp threads with the other. As the weaving progresses, the clamps and the leashes can be moved to new positions higher up the frame.

Continuous looped leashes
In the continuous method, small loops for threading onto the dowel rod are tied at regular intervals in the cotton twine used for the leashes. Make pairs of marks 100 mm (4 in.) apart every 600 mm (24 in.) using a felt-tipped marker. Bring each pair of marks together and tie a knot to make an overhand loop in the twine, figure 2.20. Two loops more than half the number of warp threads will be required, one extra for each side of the warp. Starting at the left hand side of the warp, weave the knotted twine through the threads under those that are behind the shed stick and over those that are in front of the shed stick. One loop must lie on top of each thread that is over the shed stick, with one left at each side of the warp. Working from the right, and with the dowel rod in the right hand, pick up the first (outside) loop on the rod and continue to pick up the loops in turn across the warp, finishing with the outside loop at the left selvedge. Check that the set of threads that lie under the shed stick have all been encircled by a loop of the leash twine, figure 2.21. Tie a length of twine from end to end of the leash rod to prevent the loops from sliding off, and finally tie the rod to the long screws of the G-clamp.

Pegging the frame
This is an alternative to G-clamps, the leash rod being tied to wooden pegs which are set permanently in the frame, instead of to the long screws of the clamps. Holes are drilled in both sides of the frame at 300 mm (12 in.) intervals to receive 200 mm (8 in.) lengths of 15 mm ($\frac{5}{8}$ in.) dowelling. The pegs must be a firm fit in the holes to withstand the strain of raising the warp threads. Each peg must be horizontally in line with the comparable peg on the other side of the frame.

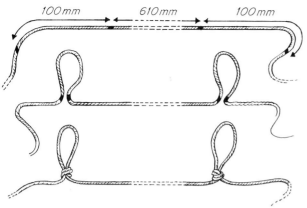

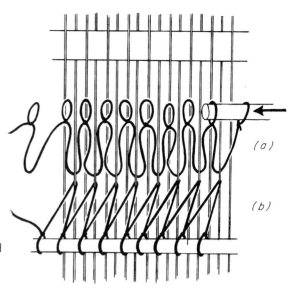

(a)

(b)

2.20 Tying leashes with continuous thread

2.21 *Right* Continuously looped thread placed on dowling rod

Frame 3 Tensioned warp *Twisted cord*

Timber requirements
Six pieces of timber are required*
2 lengths A and B 900 mm x 50 mm x 50 mm (36 in. x 2 in. x 2 in.)
4 lengths C, D, E, F 900 mm x 50 mm x 25 mm (36 in. x 2 in. x 1 in.)
also
one shed stick 900 mm x 25 mm x 5 mm (36 in. x 1 in. x $\frac{3}{16}$ in.)
one leash rod 900 mm x 10 mm x 10 mm (36 in. x $\frac{1}{2}$ in. x $\frac{1}{2}$ in.)
two warp sticks 1.1 mm x 20 mm x 20 mm (38 in. x $\frac{3}{4}$ in. x $\frac{3}{4}$ in.)

Construction
As frame 2

Threading up the frame
Frame 3 can be supported on a table for use while sitting down. It is 900 mm (36 in.) square and can accommodate a small rug of 750 mm x 1150 mm (30 in. x 48 in.), figure 2.22.

A tensioning device enables the warp threads to be tightened or relaxed mechanically. In this frame the tensioning is done with twisted cords. The cords are arranged at 100 mm - 150 mm (4 in. - 6 in.) intervals between the two warp sticks on which the warp threads are strung.

There are several differences in the method of setting up this frame compared with the previous ones.

1 The frame should be marked off as before, on the top and bottom bars, for 380 mm (15 in.) either side of the centre, to make a 750 mm (30 in.) wide warp. For 16 ends per 100 mm (4 ends per inch) mark off 5 mm ($\frac{1}{4}$ in.) intervals, for 24 ends per 100 mm (6 ends per inch) mark off 4 mm ($\frac{1}{16}$ in.) intervals.

---

*The metric and imperial measurements are not exact equivalents but are convenient sizes in each system. Do not mix the systems.

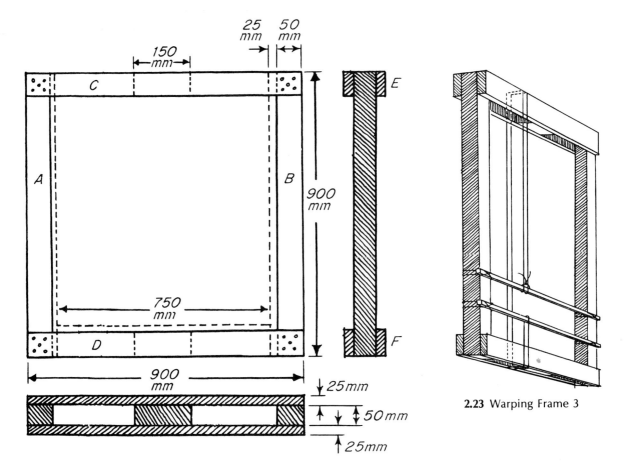

2.23 Warping Frame 3

2.22 Frame 3 (tensioned warp) – twisted cord

2 Two warp sticks, each 20 mm (³/₄ in.) square and 50 mm (2 in.) longer than the width of the frame, (ie 1.1 m (38 in.)) are required. They are tied firmly to the back of the side members of the frame, about 150 mm (6 in.) apart and parallel to the bottom bars, figure 2.23.

3 The warp is made up of individual lengths of thread instead of being in one continuous length. A double thread twice the length of the frame is required. Starting in the centre and working out to either side, loop the thread round the lower warp stick, bring it down under the bottom of the frame, up over the top, and down again to the upper warp stick, tying the ends in a reef knot, figure 2.24. This will make two single warp ends, which should be positioned over the marks on the top and bottom bars. The outside selvedge threads must again be doubled. When the warp is complete, the tension must be checked. Loosen the knots of any tight or slack threads, adjust the tension and re-tie the knot.

Cord tensioner

A medium-fine strong cord is required, such as linen loom cord, which is ideal for the purpose. The cords must be long enough to go round both warp sticks and have ends long enough to be tied under tension with a reef knot, figure 2.25(a). The cords should be spaced at about 100 mm - 150 mm (4 in. - 6 in.) intervals, and each

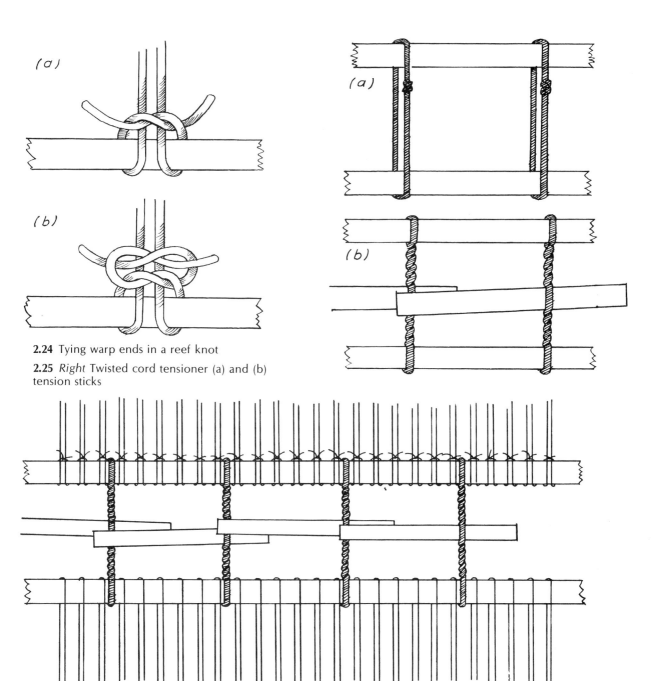

2.24 Tying warp ends in a reef knot

2.25 *Right* Twisted cord tensioner (a) and (b) tension sticks

2.26 General view of warp and tensioned cords

cord will need a tension stick measuring one and one half times the distance between the cords, in length. One end of the stick is placed in the middle of the loop, and the other end is taken round in a circle to twist the cord up and apply the tension, figure 2.25(b). Before cutting the strings holding the warp sticks in position, twist the tension cords a few times to take up the strain, resting the longer end of the stick against the next cord to prevent it from untwisting, figure 2.26. Then remove the strings holding the warp sticks in position, and bring the warp up to weaving tension, having previously moved the lower warp stick to the bottom of the frame to reduce the amount of waste in the warp.

Turn the frame round so that the tensioner is at the back, and pick up the two sheds ready for weaving as described for frame 2.

Finally weave a small heading before starting on the rug itself. This can be either a few rows of plain weave in thick waste yarn, or two or three strips of cardboard 900 mm x 40 mm (36 in. x 1½ in.). In either case, a firm base is provided on which to start weaving.

Frame 4 Tensioned warp *Bolt mechanism figure 2.27*

Timber requirements*
2 side pieces A and B 1750 mm x 50 mm x 50 mm (72 in. x 2 in. x 2 in.)
4 top and bottom pieces C, D, E, F, 1300 mm x 25 mm x 50 mm (50 in. x 1 in. x 2 in.)
2 strengthening pieces top and bottom 450 mm x 50 mm x 50 mm (18 in. x 2 in. x 2 in.)
2 pieces for tensioner 1150 mm x 50 mm x 25 mm (44 in. x 2 in. x 1 in.)
2 warp sticks 1150 mm x 25 mm x 25 mm (44 in. x 1 in. x 1 in.)
1 shed stick 1300 mm x 50 mm x 5 mm (50 in. x 1½ in. x ³⁄₁₆ in.)
1 leash rod 1300 mm x 25 mm x 25 mm (50 in. x 1 in. x 1 in.)

Hardware
3 - 250 mm to 300 mm (10 in. to 12 in.) cup square or carriage bolts
24 - 50 mm (2 in.) x 6's or 8's screws
This is a large frame to weave rugs of up to 1800 mm x 1120 mm (72 in. x 44 in.)

Construction
Construction is similar to that of frame 2.

Place the two long pieces A and B 1300 mm (50 in.) apart and screw C and E to the top, back and front. Measure 1300 mm (50 in.) from the top and screw D and F to the uprights, back and front, leaving 450 mm (18 in.) legs on which the frame will stand. 50 mm (2 in.) screws should be used and countersunk, with at least three screws at each corner. The legs make the frame a more convenient height for weaving.

The bolt tensioner
The tensioner for this frame is constructed from two pieces of timber 1150 mm x 50 mm x 25 mm (44 in. x 2 in. x 1 in.). Drill three corresponding holes large enough to take the bolts in both pieces of timber, and smaller holes at approximately 150 mm (6 in.) intervals between the holes for the bolts. Insert the bolts into both pieces simultaneously, put on the washers and the wing nuts and

*The metric and imperial measurements are not exact equivalents but are convenient sizes in each system. Do not mix the systems.

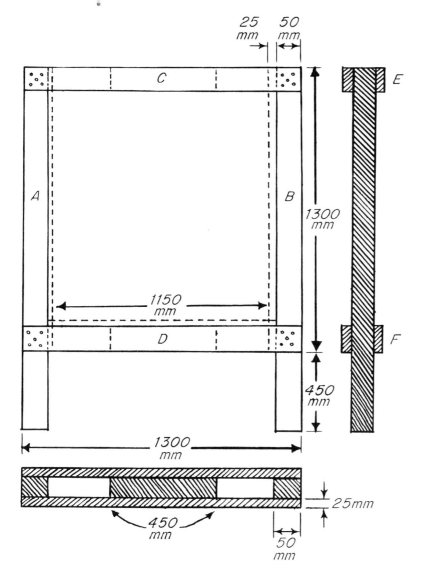

2.27 Frame 4 (tensioned warp) – bolt mechanism

screw the nuts down for about 25 mm (1 in.) figure 2.28. The thread on the bolt must be at least half the length of the bolt. The warp sticks are attached to the tension bars by loops of strong cord. Drive two nails into a block of wood, about 200 mm (8 in.) apart. Cut the cords about 500 mm (20 in.) long for the loops, and then

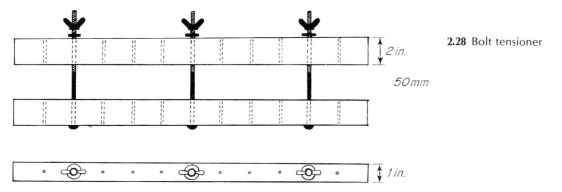

2.28 Bolt tensioner

tie each one round the nails in turn, so that they are all of equal length.

Thread the loops through the tension bars from the middle outwards, putting brass washers on the cords by the knots to prevent the loops from pulling through the holes when the cord stretches and the knots settle. Lastly, pass the warp sticks through their respective loops in turn. It is essential that the cords are all equal in length, so that the tension is even, figure 2.29.

Warping
The frame should be marked off from the centre on the top and bottom bars (C and D) as before. The warping method is similar to that of frame 3, except that as the warp sticks and the tensioner are not long enough to be secured to the sides of the frame, they are tied to the top and bottom instead, figure 2.30. When warping on a frame of this size, it is better to secure it firmly in a position convenient for the weaver. It is sometimes easier to work from the side of the loom, completing one half of the warp before turning the loom round to do the other half. Cut double lengths of thread for the warp, twice the height of the square of the frame, and thread up as in frame 3, taking the thread right round the frame to tie to the upper warp stick as in figure 2.23.

When the warping is completed, cut the strings holding the tensioner in position and move it down so that the warp stick is level with the base of the frame, so that the amount of waste is kept to a minimum.

Insert a shed stick in the threads on the face of the loom, and set up the leashes on the dowel rod as for frame 2.

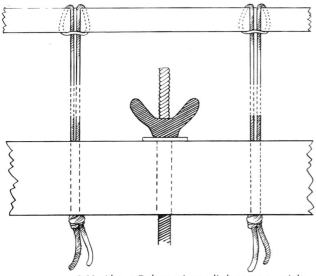

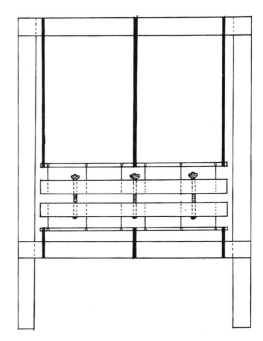

2.29 *Above* Bolt tensioner link to warp sticks

2.30 Tensioner held in position by strings secured to the top and bottom bars

3 THE LOOM

Looms vary considerably in size and shape, but they all fall into one of two categories, foot-power looms or table looms. There is one common factor: they all hold the warp under tension while the shafts separate the warp threads into two layers to form the shed.

The best looms for rug weaving are the foot-power looms. Table looms are, on the whole, designed for lighter warps, but it is possible to use a sturdy model for weaving rug samples, provided that the tension of the warp is not too great. Generally, however, table looms are neither wide nor strong enough for rug making, and the batten is not sufficiently strong and heavy enough to beat up the thick materials required for rugs. To maintain an even tension across the whole width of the warp, a rug loom must be completely rigid at all times, and it must also be capable of supporting a heavy batten.

Floor looms can be divided into two groups; upright, figure 3.1, and horizontal, figure 3.2. It will be seen that the named parts are identical in both looms, only the position of the parts has been re-arranged to suit the change of direction of the warp. The main advantage of the upright loom is that it requires less floor space, and another advantage is that it is possible to stand back away from the loom and assess the design from a distance. On the other hand, it is slower to operate, and is usually constructed with only two shafts, which limits the range of woven structures. It is also more difficult to pass the weft from side to side through the shed.

Horizontal floor looms can carry up to twelve shafts, controlled by treadles, hence the name 'foot-power loom'. The weft can be passed from side to side more quickly and easily, and the over-slung batten, hanging from the frame, is much more effective than the sliding batten on the upright loom, and, for that matter, than the underslung batten used on some foot-power looms.

Horizontal foot-power loom

The loom consists of a strong, rectangular wooden frame which carries the working parts. The two side frames are connected by several cross-members, three of which are used to guide the warp between the two rollers. The others are tie-beams, two of which serve the dual purpose of carrying the treadles and the mounting

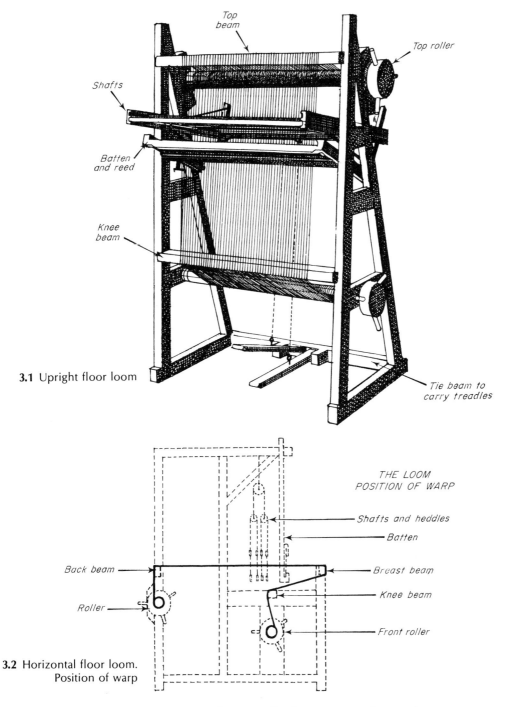

3.1 Upright floor loom

Labels on figure 3.1:
- Top beam
- Top roller
- Shafts
- Batten and reed
- Knee beam
- Tie beam to carry treadles

3.2 Horizontal floor loom. Position of warp

Labels on figure 3.2:
- THE LOOM POSITION OF WARP
- Shafts and heddles
- Batten
- Back beam
- Breast beam
- Roller
- Knee beam
- Front roller

respectively as well, figure 3.3. The various parts are described below.

Beams

The three beams that guide the warp are the back beam, and the breast beam, which are at the two horizontal extremes of the warp, and the knee beam, which carries the cloth away from the

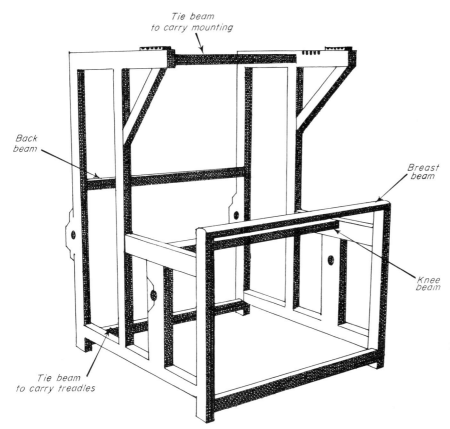

Tie beam to carry mounting

Back beam

Breast beam

Knee beam

Tie beam to carry treadles

3.3 Horizontal floor loom. Wooden frame including beams

weaver's knees as it passes downward from the breast beam to the cloth roller. These beams are frequently dove-tailed into the frames of the loom, but the breast beam may be tenoned or tusk tenoned instead. All three beams can be removed from the loom without difficulty for threading or tying up and the stability of the loom is unaffected.

Rollers

There are two rollers, the warp roller at the rear of the loom and the cloth roller at the front, figure 3.4. The warp roller is usually, though not necessarily, mounted below the back beam, and from it the warp unwinds over the back beam and forwards through the harness to the front of the loom. The cloth roller accepts the woven cloth from the breast beam via the knee beam. The rollers are a minimum of 100 mm (4 in.) diameter, and are usually between 150 mm (6 in.) and 200 mm (8 in.) diameter. They can be turned to a circular section, or planed to an octagonal section, and can also be fabricated from a small square-section beam with four rectangular lengths attached to the faces to make a cruciform-section roller. The two ends are turned down to form pivots about 50 mm (2 in.) diameter which run in holes in the side frame of the loom. Each roller has a ratchet wheel of wood or metal at one end, and, on the same end, a handle to turn it with, figure 3.5. Pawls, usually one, but sometimes two, are fastened to the side frame

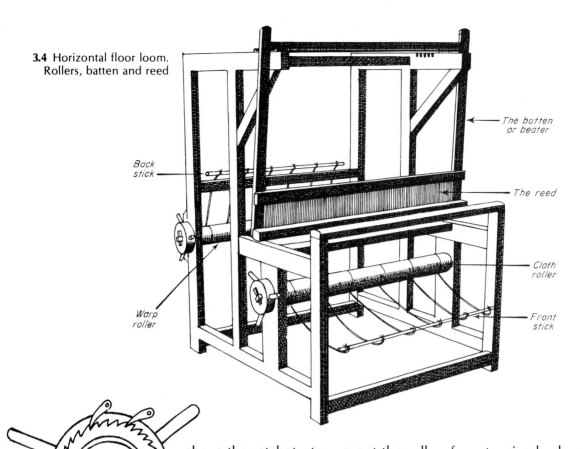

3.4 Horizontal floor loom.
Rollers, batten and reed

The batten
or beater

The reed

Back
stick

Cloth
roller

Warp
roller

Front
stick

3.5 Ratchet wheel and
metal pawls

above the ratchets, to prevent the rollers from turning backwards
when the warp is under tension. Rollers are sometimes referred to
as beams, but confusion can then arise between the warp roller
and the warp beam.

Batten or beater

This is the name given to the movable wooden frame carrying the
reed, figure 3.4. It is hung from the top of the loom (overslung),
and is swung by the weaver to strike the fell of the cloth to compact the weft yarns.

Shafts and heddles

The heddles are loops of twine, with two large loops either side
of a central eye, through which the warp yarn is threaded. They
are threaded onto two shaft sticks at the top and bottom, figure
3.6, and the complete unit is usually called a *shaft*, though there
are other terms, such as *stave, harness, leaf,* etc. A complete set
of shafts is called a *harness,* and the whole of the movable mechanism for shedding, ie dividing the warp threads, is called the
mounting. The shafts are suspended from the top of the loom
and positioned about half way between the back beam and the
batten to give maximum shed with the minimum of strain on
the warp.

String heddles can be made quite easily from cotton twine by

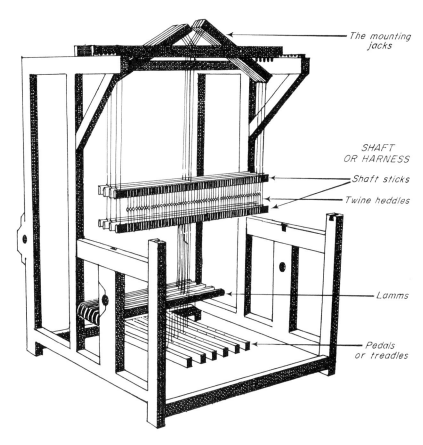

The mounting jacks

SHAFT OR HARNESS

Shaft sticks

Twine heddles

Lamms

Pedals or treadles

3.6 Horizontal floor loom. Position of shafts and mounting

tying the loops round a set of four nails which have been driven into a block of wood at the correct spacing and the heads removed. Heddles of wire are frequently used for fine weaving, but are not as convenient as string heddles for rugs.

Shedding
There are two basic types of shedding, that in which some of the threads are moved away from the centre line of the shed, and that in which all the threads are moved one way or the other. The choice of shedding motion is to some extent determined by the type of fabric being woven, as the unbalanced shed puts a considerable strain on the warp threads that are moved, while the balanced shed creates less strain and distributes it evenly across the warp. As rug warps are inelastic and comparatively heavy, the balanced shed is more suitable for rug weaving.

Both the countermarch and the counterbalanced systems give balanced sheds. A countermarch loom can carry twelve or sixteen shafts and shed perfectly all the time. Counterbalanced looms, on the other hand, are limited usually to four shafts. There are various types of shedding mechanism, using rollers, pulleys or heddle-horses.

Pedals or treadles
These are wooden levers operated by the feet to raise or lower

the shafts. It is better to have the pedals pivoted at the back of the loom, figure 3.6, to give a better system of leverage and so make it easier to open a wide shed.

Front and back sticks

These are for tying the warp onto the front and back rollers, and are attached to the rollers by a lacing of cord or by a canvas apron, figure 3.4. The sticks must be strong and rigid enough to remain straight under tension. Whether cords or a canvas apron are used, the sticks must be parallel to the beams of the loom before starting to weave.

The counterbalanced loom

In this type of loom, as its name implies, shafts are balanced one against the other, or one pair against another pair, so that as one set sinks the other rises. The original, and the simplest, method of doing this is to tie a single shaft to each end of a short length of wood which is supported by a cord from the top of the loom. When one shaft is sunk the other is raised. This is the minimum harness of two shafts, and to expand it into four shafts, the length of wood supporting the first pair of shafts is balanced against a similar length supporting the second pair, either with a third length of wood or over a pulley, figure 3.7(a). These lengths of wood, or heddle-horses, can be replaced by pulleys to make a more compact harness, figure 3.7(b), or by rollers to make a more efficient harness, figure 3.7(c).

The bottom sticks of the shafts are tied to levers running across the loom, the lamms or marches, and these are tied to the treadles running from back to front of the loom, figure 3.8. In this way, any treadle can be tied to any shaft via its lamm, and combinations of

3.7 Counterbalanced loom. Shaft lifting mechanisms (a), (b) and (c)

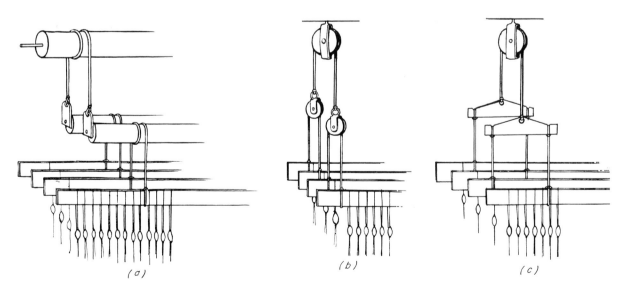

(a)   (b)   (c)

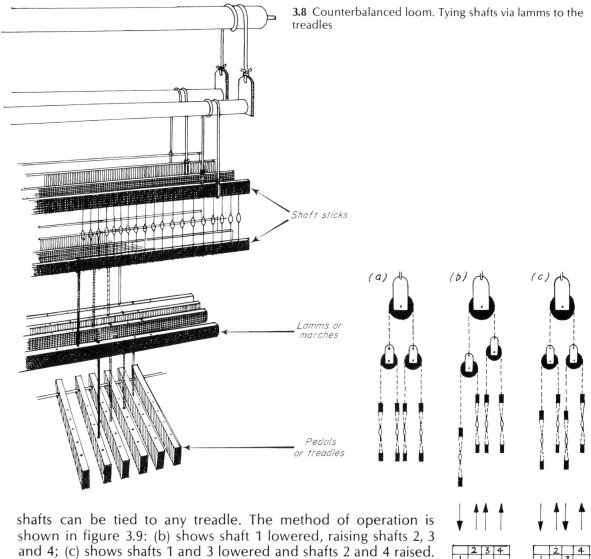

3.8 Counterbalanced loom. Tying shafts via lamms to the treadles

Shaft sticks

Lamms or marches

Pedals or treadles

(a)   (b)   (c)

3.9 Counterbalanced loom. Method of operation

shafts can be tied to any treadle. The method of operation is shown in figure 3.9: (b) shows shaft 1 lowered, raising shafts 2, 3 and 4; (c) shows shafts 1 and 3 lowered and shafts 2 and 4 raised. For a plain weave, with a straight threading, 1, 2, 3, 4, the two sheds will be 1 and 3, 2 and 4, the odd numbered shafts being lowered on one shed and the even numbered on the other.

The countermarch loom

In the harness of a countermarch loom there are separate systems for raising and lowering the shafts, so that both the rising and the sinking sheds can be adjusted individually. The shafts are suspended from the outer ends by pairs of horizontal jacks or coupers, and long cords from the inner ends of the jacks go down to the long marches below the shafts, figure 3.10. Sinking a long march pulls down the inner ends of the jacks tied to it, so the outer ends rise and lift the shaft. Below the shafts are the short marches or countermarches, which are tied directly to the lower shaft sticks. When one of these is sunk, it takes down the shaft which is tied to it. With certain rare exceptions, every shaft has to be tied to rise or sink on each treadle.

The cording of a mounting is from the top downwards. First the jacks are pegged horizontally, and the inner ends of each pair joined by a length of single or doubled cord threaded down through one jack and up through the other, making a loop of about 125 mm (5 in.) below the jacks, figure 3.11. Suspend the shafts from the top of the loom with the eyes on the warp line, and run doubled cords from the outer ends of the jacks to the ends of the shafts, using an adjusting knot, figure 3.12. Loop a doubled cord over the short cord joining the pairs of jacks, figure 3.13, pass it down behind its shaft, and fasten it to its march with an adjusting knot. Finally tie the lower shaft sticks to the counter-marches with the adjusting knot. Stretch all the cords to settle the knots, and re-check all the adjustments, making sure that the shafts are still on the warp line and the short countermarches and the long marches are horizontal. The cording from the marches and countermarches to the treadles varies according to the pattern or the type of weave required. Each shaft has to be tied to rise or sink on each treadle. If the loom has two sets of marches on separate spindles, it is usually easier to tie all the rising ties on the lower marches first, and then all the sinking ties on the upper marches, but if the loom has all the marches and countermarches on one spindle it is better to tie all the ties in order, one treadle at a time.

To maintain an even shed, the back shafts must move further from the warp line than the front shafts, so the back ties must be shorter than the front ties. Back-slung treadles are mechanically easier to operate than front-slung treadles, but as the amount of travel is greater in the front, ie the complete opposite of the requirements for a good shed, the back ties on this type of loom need to be even shorter than on a loom with front-slung treadles.

The weaver's weight is thrown forward when the shuttle is thrown, so the treadles should be firmly on the floor when the sheds are fully open. With the treadle down, the back ties must be adjusted to give the correct shed, and then the other ties on the same treadle adjusted to give the same height at the reed. This means that the shafts are not level from front to back when the shed is fully open, the tops rise from the reed towards the back of the loom. The first treadle to be adjusted should be the one at the free end of the marches, as here the travel is greatest, and the limiting factor is often the marches, treadles or shafts fouling each other, the loom frame or the cloth roller. Successive treadles must be adjusted to give a shed as nearly equal as possible to the shed on the first treadle. When the locking pins in the jacks have been removed the harness drops slightly under the weight of the marches and treadles, but this does not affect the adjustment.

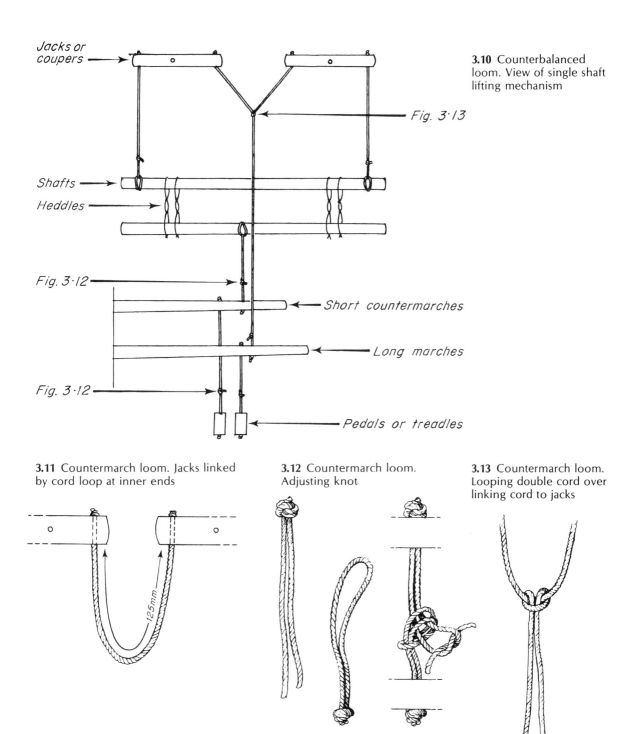

Jacks or coupers

3.10 Counterbalanced loom. View of single shaft lifting mechanism

Fig. 3·13

Shafts

Heddles

Fig. 3·12

Short countermarches

Long marches

Fig. 3·12

Pedals or treadles

3.11 Countermarch loom. Jacks linked by cord loop at inner ends

125 mm

3.12 Countermarch loom. Adjusting knot

3.13 Countermarch loom. Looping double cord over linking cord to jacks

4 THE WARP

Warps can be wound to any required length, as determined by the size of the rug or rugs and the number to be woven on the same warp. Occasionally, the width of the loom may be a deciding factor.

Unless a rug is designed for a narrow place, such as a corridor or landing, the proportions can vary from a square to a long rectangle. The length of the warp is calculated to include not only the length of the rug itself, but take-up in the weaving, and wastage at both ends of the warp. The take-up is approximately 10 to 12 per cent of the total woven length, ie about 100 mm to the metre (1 in. to the foot). The waste at the beginning of the warp is about 300 mm (12 in.) and at the end almost twice this amount, 450 mm - 600 mm (18 in. - 24 in.).

Warps for sampling

A practical size for a sampling warp is about 300 mm (12 in.) wide, and long enough for six square samples. This is economical in the use of materials, but at the same time large enough for representative samples to be woven. Space must be left between the samples for finishing the warp ends with knots or fringes, and this is also about 300 mm (12 in.). To this must be added the waste at the ends of the warp, totalling about 1 m (36 in.). The following example gives the length of warp for six 300 mm (12 in.) samples.

6 samples of 300 mm (12 in.) =	1800 mm (72 in.)
5 spaces of 300 mm (12 in.) =	1525 mm (60 in.)
front waste (knots) =	305 mm (12 in.)
back waste (shedding) =	610 mm (24 in.)
	4240 mm (168 in.)

These calculations are on the whole generous, and would allow for 10 per cent take-up.

Winding the warp

The easiest way to set the moveable pegs on a warping mill or a board to the required length of warp is to tie a loop in the end of a length of yarn, measure the length for the warp and mark it with another knot or a felt-tipped pen, place the loop over the first peg and wind the measuring thread down the mill or board. The peg for the end of the warp is then placed in the next possible hole beyond the knot, unless, of course, the knot is only just beyond the previous hole, and a short length can be left off the warp. If warps are made fairly frequently, it is worth while making a permanent measuring thread. Tie the loop at the end, and a large knot at every metre (yard) for five or six metres (yards). The second half of the thread can have a small knot at the half-metre (half-yard) intervals between the metre (yard) marks. This is sufficiently accurate, as the spaces between the pegs are usually too large to allow an absolutely exact length of warp to be made, and small distances can be estimated. Most mills and boards have a set of two or three fixed pegs at the top or at a corner respectively, on which to make the cross. Making a cross at the moveable end often results in unnecessary waste. Figure 4.1(a) and (b) shows two methods of winding the warp on a warping board.

4.1 (a and b) Two methods of winding the warp on a warping board

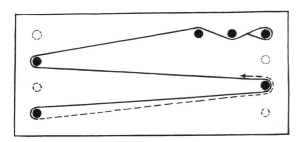 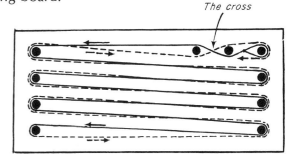

The cross

The cross is essential to keep the threads in the order in which they were wound, and to prevent tangling. The cross is made on two pegs, the yarns going first one way and then the other alternately as they pass between the pegs, figure 4.2(a). Between each pair of threads going the same way, there is always one thread going the opposite way, which stops them crossing over each other. Warps must be wound with a light, even tension and, if necessary, a wide warp should be made in sections to prevent a build-up of thread which would interfere with the evenness of tension. The sections are later placed together on the cross sticks. If the yarn needs to be joined, this should be done behind a peg, at one end or the other, as a knot in the warp will make weaving difficult and may also cause a fault to show in the fabric. It is better to start and finish at the end away from the cross, to save having loose ends which can become entangled in the warp and may not be caught onto the warp stick. The beginning and end of the warp should each be tied in a loop, which is placed on the end peg.

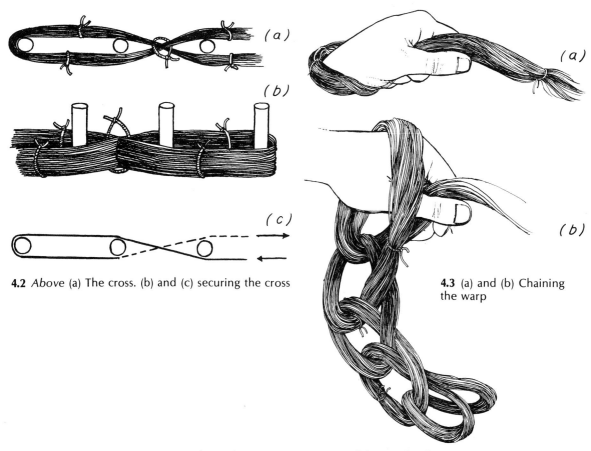

4.2 *Above* (a) The cross. (b) and (c) securing the cross

4.3 (a) and (b) Chaining the warp

Before the warp is removed from the board, the cross must be secured by tying it with lengths of strong cord or thread. One length goes round the cross itself, and four more are tied around the arms of the cross, figure 4.2(b). The warp must next be tied round at intervals of 500 mm (18 in.) throughout its length, preferably with a thread of contrasting colour. Should the warp be long, it can be reduced to a more manageable size by chaining it from the end away from the cross, figure 4.3. It can now be removed from the mill in safety, and transferred to the loom.

Raddling the warp

First remove the batten and the reed from the loom, and clear the centre of the loom by moving the heddles along the shafts to the sides. Thread the cross onto the cross sticks, and tie the sticks together at the ends, figure 4.4. Remove the warp stick from the loom, thread it through the end loop of the warp, and re-tie the outside cords only, to secure it to the warp roller. The threads securing the cross and those adjacent to it can now be removed.

Fasten the raddle, with its cap or top removed, securely across the loom at some point between the shafts and the back beam. Bring the warp forward over the raddle and work the cross sticks

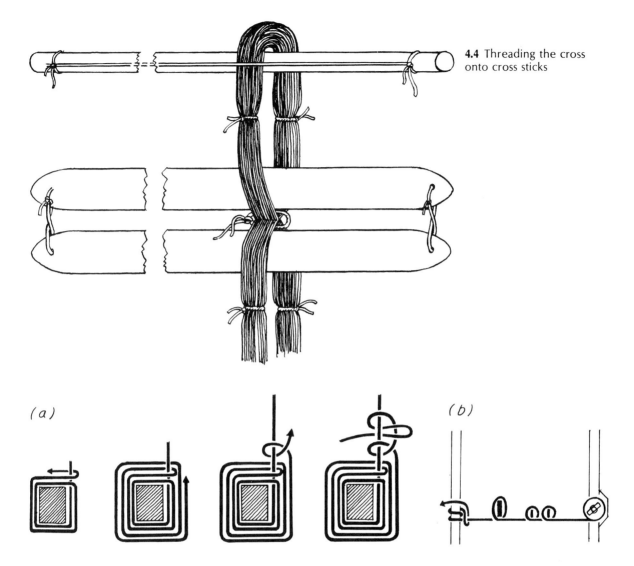

4.4 Threading the cross onto cross sticks

(a)   *(b)*

4.5 (a) Knot for right hand upright (b) Two cords holding cross sticks and raddle in position on the loom

down till they are near the back of the raddle, and tie them in this position across the loom. (If there is no convenient part of the frame of the loom to tie the sticks or raddle to, fasten a length of strong cord to each side of the back beam of the loom, bring each one forward and round the two cross sticks and the bottom of the raddle in turn and finally tie them to their respective front uprights of the loom.) Tension can be applied to a cord such as this by pulling it firmly and taking the end twice round the upright in one direction, round itself and back twice in the other direction, applying the full tension as the end is taken backwards for the first reverse turn. Finish the knot by taking the end once more round the cord, up inside the loop, pull taut and add a slip loop, figure 4.5. Only a strong cord such as linen loom cord will stand this treatment. Divide the warp at the centre and lay the two halves at the ends of the raddle, placing a folded sheet of newspaper over the teeth of the raddle to stop the warp falling into

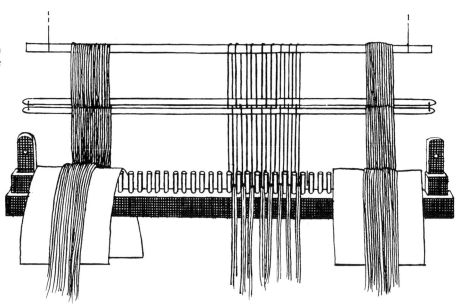

the dents. Working from the centre outwards, take the threads from the centre of the cross in the order in which they were warped and place them in the teeth of the raddle according to the sett of the warp, figure 4.6. Dents in the raddle usually vary from 10 to 15 dents per 100 mm (2 to 4 dents per inch), so the dentage of the warp will have to be calculated. It may involve a slightly irregular grouping of the threads, such as 2, 3, 2, 3, or 3, 0, 2, 0, etc. As soon as the threading is complete, replace the cap of the raddle and fasten it securely, tying it on with thread round the ends if there are no pegs. Next spread the warp evenly across the warp stick at the back of the loom. At this stage the warp stick will be held only by the two outside cords. Pulling the warp forward until the stick touches the back of the raddle will automatically spread the warp. Then tie the remainder of the cords onto the warp stick.

Warping the beam – single handed

This is not a difficult operation, but takes longer than with an assistant. The small loops tying the warp together must be undone and the warp shaken out to spread it more easily and to prevent the formation of tangles. Loop the warp round the breast beam and rotate the warp roller once without applying tension. The warp must then be tightened round the roller by picking up 6 to 8 threads in turn and pulling each group with equal force right across the warp. Give the roller one complete turn and repeat the process. As the warp builds up on the roller, insert warp sticks or folded newspaper between the layers of threads to prevent uneven tension. As the warp is wound on, the cross sticks have to be moved down the warp. When the end of the warp has reached the breast beam, move the cross sticks back to the back beam and tie them into place across the loom with twine. Cut the front warp loops with scissors ready for threading the heddles and the reed.

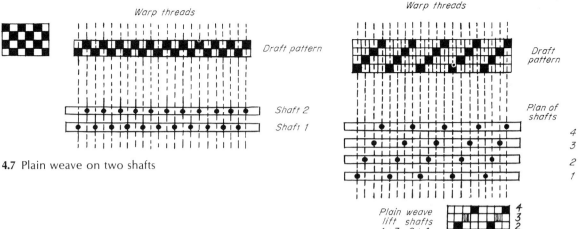

4.7 Plain weave on two shafts

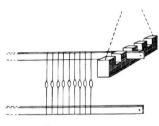

4.8 Plain weave on four shafts

Threading the warp

The order of threading to be used is determined by the pattern of the weave. Plain weave is usually threaded on two shafts, the warp threads passing through the eyes on each shaft alternately, figure 4.7. Plain weave can also be threaded on four shafts in a straight draft, ie 1, 2, 3, 4. In this threading, the shafts are lifted in pairs 1 and 3 and 2 and 4, figure 4.8. This threading is required on counterbalanced looms when all four shafts are in use.

To be able to thread easily and accurately, the shafts must be held rigidly and slightly apart from each other. Castles, figure 4.9, are simple items of equipment specially designed for the purpose, but although they are a considerable help, they are not an essential. In their absence, the shafts can be held by taking a length of loom cord round the end of each shaft in turn and then round all four shafts together, tying it securely away from the heddles. When this has been done at both ends, the top shaft sticks can be slipped into loops of cord and suspended from the top of the loom.

Ensure that the heddles on each side of the shafts are equal in number. Divide the warp into equal parts, and, starting from the centre, take the first thread from the cross. The warp is drawn through the heddle eyes with a threading hook. Both halves of the warp are threaded from the centre outwards, the left half being threaded *backwards*, 2, 1, 2, 1 . . . and the right half *forwards*, 1, 2, 1, 2 . . . to ensure the correct sequence of threading. The last heddles on each side will be threaded double to strengthen the selvedge. As the threading progresses, the warp threads should be tied together in small groups of about six or eight ends with a slip knot, to prevent the threads from being pulled accidently from the heddles, figure 4.10(a), (b) and (c).

Replace the batten in the loom, and tie it firmly to the sides to stop it moving, and place in a reed of the correct dentage. Using a reed hook, start again from the centre and draw the threads through the dents of the reed in the order in which they were threaded through the heddles, tying the threads in small groups again for safety.

4.9 Castles

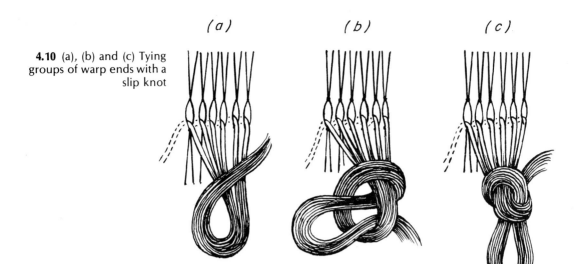

4.10 (a), (b) and (c) Tying groups of warp ends with a slip knot

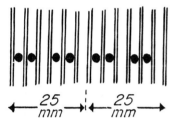

4.11 Using reed for different warp setting

Reeds can be used for setts other than those for which they were made. For example 18 ends per 100 mm can be threaded on a 24s reed (4 ends per inch in a 6s reed), figure 4.11. Dents can be missed without harm: 2, 2, 0, is quicker to thread than 2, 1, 1, to put four ends into three dents and just as efficient. Alternate dents can be missed in a reed of twice the required sett, and threads can be doubled up in a reed of half the sett. Yarns must be able to move freely in the dents of the reed, so care must be taken to ensure that too fine a reed for the weight of the yarn is not used, or that thick yarns are not doubled up in a fine reed.

Tying to the front stick

Tying the threads to the front stick should be carried out in the following way.

1 Working again from the centre of the warp, take 8 to 10 threads and draw them through the fingers to ensure equal tension and correct order.

2 Bring the threads over the front stick, divide them into two sections, figure 4.12(a), and pass them down under the rod and up outside the original group of threads.

3 Knot the ends together over the top of the group of threads with half a reef knot, figure 4.12(b).

4 Tie the remainder of the warp similarly, taking bunches from alternate sides to maintain an even tension on the warp.

Check the threads with the tips of the fingers for evenness of tension, and adjust where necessary, simply lifting the knot towards the reed and re-tightening when the threads are slack, which is usually the case. Finish each bunch in turn by adding the second half of the reef knot, figure 4.12(c).

Before removing the ties that are keeping the shafts and batten located, check that the pedals and lamms are correctly tied.

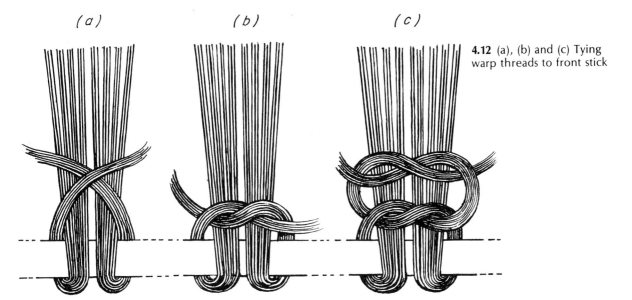

4.12 (a), (b) and (c) Tying warp threads to front stick

Opening out the knot groups

Before starting to weave, adjust the position of the front warp stick till the reed can beat firmly against it, and then bring the warp up to tension without altering that position by turning both front and back rollers a little at a time.

To open out the groups of threads, weave six or eight picks in a thick yarn and beat down well after each pick, if necessary beating twice, with the shed changed for the second beat.

Calculating quantities

To calculate the amount of yarn required for a particular piece of work, two things must be known, the total length of yarn needed, and the relationship between the weight and the length of the yarn to be used. This is called the count of the yarn, and is defined in one of two ways; by stating the weight of a fixed length of yarn, which is called the fixed length or the direct system, or by stating the length of a fixed weight of yarn, the fixed weight or the indirect system. In the direct system, the count number increases with an increase in thickness, and in the indirect system, the count number decreases with the increase in thickness. All the traditional systems, direct and indirect, are gradually being replaced by the new direct decimal system, tex, which is based on the internationally-agreed metric units, and applies to all yarns and fibres. Conversion between the various systems, and to, and from tex, is quite straightforward, and the conversion factors and standards for the different systems are given in the tables below.

Continuous filament yarns, ie thrown silk and all man-made fibres, use a direct system of counting, the denier system. When man-made fibres were first produced, they automatically followed the system of counting already in use for the only natural continuous-filament fibre, silk.

47

Most, though not all, of the spun yarns use indirect systems of counting. These were based on some fixed weight, which varied from district to district, and the count number was the number of standard length packages of yarn which together made up the standard weight. The only notable direct systems for spun yarns are the Aberdeen system for wool, dry-spun linen, hemp and jute, and the American grain system for wool. The tables below give the standard units of weight and length for the most common systems and the conversion factors to tex.

Direct systems

The count number is the weight in weight units of a standard length of the yarn.

System	Unit of length	Unit of weight	Conversion factor to tex
Tex	1000 metres	gramme	—
Denier	9000 metres	gramme	0.1111
Aberdeen jute, hemp linen (dry spun) wool	14,400 yd spindle	pound	34.45

To convert:

To tex: multiply count by conversion factor

direct count x conversion factor = tex count

From tex: divide count by conversion factor

$$\frac{\text{tex count}}{\text{conversion factor}} = \text{direct count}$$

Indirect systems

The count number is the number of standard packages which together make up one weight unit.

System	Unit of length	Unit of weight	Conversion factor to tex
Cotton	840 yd hank	1 pound	590.5
Woollen			
Galashiels	300 yd cut	24 ounces (=200 yd/lb)	2480
Yorkshire skein	256 yd skein	1 pound	1938
American cut	300 yd cut	1 pound	1654
American run	100 yd run	1 ounce	310
Worsted	560 yd hank	1 pound	885.8
Linen (wet spun)	300 yd lea	1 pound	1654
Silk, spun	840 yd hank	1 pound	590.5
Metric	1000 metres	1 kilogramme	1000

To convert:

To tex: divide conversion factor by count

$$\frac{\text{conversion factor}}{\text{indirect count}} = \text{tex count}$$

From tex: divide conversion factor by count

$$\frac{\text{conversion factor}}{\text{tex count}} = \text{indirect count}$$

To find the weight of the warp required for a particular piece of work, the total length of warp yarn must be calculated, by multiplying the number of threads in the warp by the length of one thread, allowing about 25 per cent extra for take-up and shrinkage, etc. This amount is then divided by the unit of length in a direct system to find the number of units required, and multiplied by the count to give the weight of the yarn needed.

$$\frac{\text{length in metres x tex count}}{1000} = \text{weight in grammes}$$

In an indirect system, the total length is divided by both the unit of length *and* by the tex count.

$$\frac{\text{length in yards}}{\text{standard length x indirect count}} = \text{weight (number of units of weight)}$$

In both systems, the count refers to the actual count of the yarn. Most yarns are plied, the main exceptions being woollens used for tweeds and some thick singles rug wools. The count of the plied yarn always indicates the number of plies in the yarn, and this must be converted into a final or resultant count for the purpose of calculation. In the tex system, the count of plied yarns can be given in two different ways, either by the prefix 'R' (for resultant count) followed by the count of the final yarn and then the ply, eg R 60 tex/2, or by giving the count of the component yarns and then the number of plies, eg 30 tex x 2. Both examples indicate a 2-ply yarn of 60s final count. In the traditional indirect system the number of plies and the count of the component yarns are usually given, in the form plies/count or count/plies, eg 2/5s or 5/2, both meaning that two fives yarns have been plied together, to give a final yarn of $2\frac{1}{2}$ count, the number of plies always being divided into the count of the component yarn. To take an example of a calculation in both systems, a total warp length of 250 m (250 yd) in a linen yarn of 600 tex (3 lea) is assumed.

Tex   *Linen count*

$$\frac{\text{length}}{\text{standard}} \times \text{count} \qquad\qquad \frac{\text{length}}{\text{standard} \times \text{count}}$$

$$\frac{250 \text{ m}}{1000} \times 600 = 150 \text{ gm} \qquad \frac{250 \text{ yd}}{300 \times 3} = 0.28 \text{ lb } (4\frac{1}{2} \text{ oz})$$

If the count of the yarn is not known, a skein can be weighed, and the total length calculated by multiplying the length of the skein (including both sides) by the number of threads in the skein. The total warp length required can then be divided by the length of the skein, and the result multiplied by the weight of the skein to give the total weight of the warp.

5 DRAFTS & WEAVE PLANS

The weave plan is the weaver's diagrammatical representation of the woven cloth, and together with the threading draft, and the lifting plan for a table loom or the tie-up and treadling plan for a foot-power loom, provides all the information that is necessary to weave the cloth.

As this book is concerned mainly with the opportunities available to the weaver to use a series of techniques involving the manipulation of the weft in what are otherwise plain-weave fabrics, the information on interpreting and writing drafts is kept to the minimum, and is presented in the simplest form.

The weave plans illustrated relate to specific woven samples, and are intended to assist beginners to visualise the woven cloth from the drafts. Information on the more complex weaves can be found in the advanced books on the subject.

Figure 5.1 illustrates the threading draft, weave plan and lifting plan for plain-weave on two shafts. The horizontal lines represent the picks of the weft, and the vertical lines represent the warp ends. The weave plan is at the point where the two sets of lines cross, the threading draft is at the top of the diagram, and the lifting plan is on the right. This is all the information the weaver requires. The numbers 1 and 2 in the threading draft indicate that the left thread of the pair shown goes on the front shaft, and the right thread onto the back shaft. The numbers on the horizontal lines give the order of lifting, and in the weave plan itself the two black squares show where the warp threads pass over the weft threads and the white squares where the weft threads are on top of the warp. It should be emphasised that the spacing of the warp threads in the plan is only diagrammatic, and does not relate to any set measurement. With the same threading, a warp of closely set fine threads would give a fine hard fabric, while a more open sett with heavier yarns would make a heavier, looser fabric.

In rug weaving, where a bold approach should be combined with a firmness of texture, the most common setting for plain weave is 16 ends per 100 mm (4 ends per inch). As a general guide, rug warps are usually set between 12 and 16 double ends or 24 and 32 single ends per 100 mm (3 and 4 double or 6 and 8 single ends per inch), using a medium weight yarn. In the more advanced weaves with complex designs the threading of the pattern has to be worked out accurately and positioned correctly in relation to

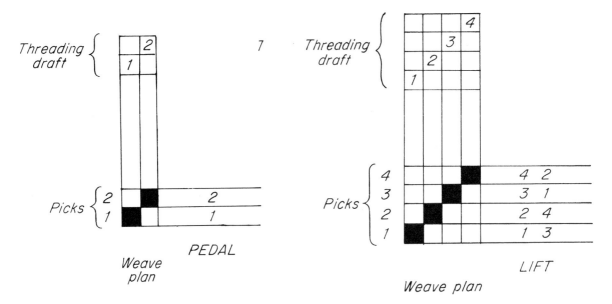

7

5.1 Weave plan – plain weave on two shafts

5.2 *Right* Weave plan – plain weave on four shafts

the warp, but in the simpler settings the warp is threaded straight through from side to side.

Figure 5.2 is the weave diagram for plain weave on a four shaft loom, such as a counterbalanced loom, which functions more efficiently with all four shafts in operation than with only two.

The last two diagrams illustrate twills on four shafts. The twill is the next development on from plain weave. The weft yarns pass over two or more adjacent warp threads, and the float of the weft moves sideways on successive picks.

The smallest possible twill is on three threads, and the weft threads go over two warp threads and under one, or *vice versa*. This gives an unbalanced twill, with a face and a back which are different. Twills on four shafts can be either balanced or unbalanced, working either two-and-two or three-and-one. The balanced twills will be the same on both sides.

For convenience, twills are referred to numerically by indicating the number of warp ends raised or lowered above and below the weft, which is shown as a short horizontal stroke, a two-and-two twill being represented by $\frac{2}{2}$ and a three-and-one twill by $\frac{3}{1}$.

Another form of this notation is 2/2 and 3/1, which, though more convenient, is not so explicit. In the chapter on *Warp-faced weaves* the two woven samples 1 and 3 vividly illustrate the effect that can be obtained by the use of a twill weave in contrast to the more straightforward plain weave.

Sample 3 illustrates the use of a $\frac{1}{3}$ twill, the weave diagram for which is given in figure 5.3. This weave, however, is not entirely satisfactory, as the unequal tension on the two sides of an unbalanced twill cause the fabric to curl at the edges. By using a $\frac{2}{2}$ twill, which is balanced, the fabric will lie flat, and will not curl.

When weaving twills for the first time, it is better to start with a weft-faced weave. In doing this, reference should be made to chapter 9, *Two, three and four shuttle techniques*, as the information in this chapter is relevant also to weaving twills in more than one colour.

A $2\over2$ weft-faced twill provides a more sophisticated surface texture than plain weave, and by the use of a second and eventually a third colour, patterns can be produced from the surface weave that are peculiar to this technique, figure 5.4.

In two, three and four shuttle techniques, much of the effect lies in the multiplicity of patterns achieved by quick shuttle changes. A $2\over2$ weft-faced twill, on the other hand, requires a much simpler and more regular sequence.

Begin by using two colours only, (a) and (b) in a predetermined sequence, ie a/a/b/a/a/b/a/a/b, etc, progressing one shaft at a time. Reversals in the pattern can be achieved by reversing the order of the shafts, eg 1 and 2, 2 and 3, 3 and 4, 4 and 1, 3 and 4, 2 and 3, etc. By using different combinations of colour, colour sequences and order of treadling, a great variety of designs is possible.

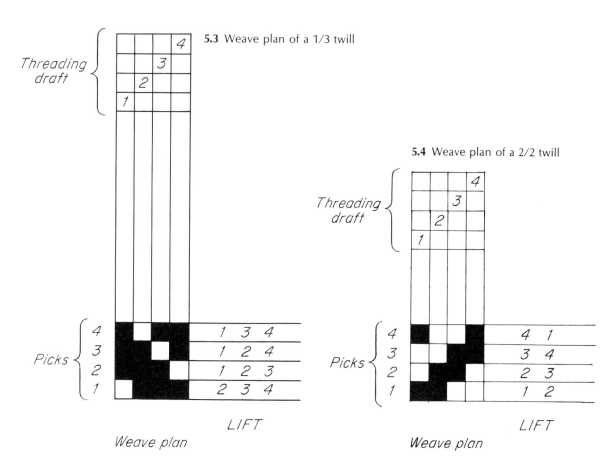

5.3 Weave plan of a 1/3 twill

5.4 Weave plan of a 2/2 twill

53

6 BEGINNING TO WEAVE

The heading

This is the beginning (and the final) edge of the rug, and is best woven as a plain strip about 50 mm (2 in.) deep. Some weavers, however, decorate the band by using a simple two shuttle pattern (see chapter 9). The heading is designed to provide a firm base upon which one of the rug finishes can be carried out.

Beginning the weft

When introducing the weft yarn into the shed for the first time it is important to avoid the doubling of the weft yarns around the warp threads, which are generally then not covered when the weft is beaten down. Yarns used in the beginning and ending of wefts should be tapered, either by the gradual shortening of a group, or in the case of a heavier yarn, the unravelling of its constituent strands or plies and again shortening by degrees. Tapering should be carried out when the yarn is placed in the shed. Individual strands can then be positioned and cut to the length required. Figure 6.1 illustrates the correct procedure in starting (and

6.1 Beginning a weft

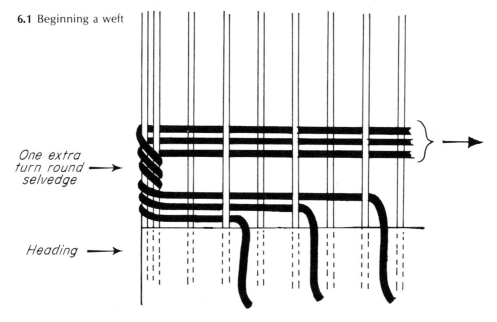

One extra
turn round
selvedge →

Heading →

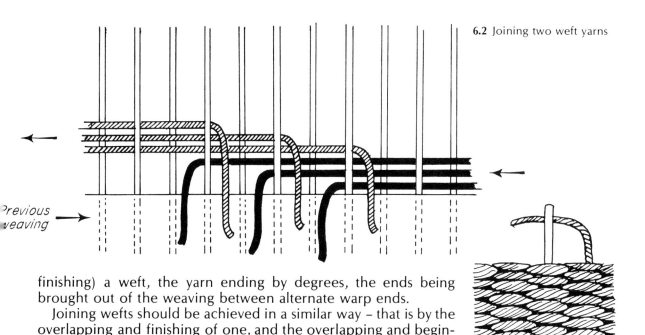

*Previous
weaving* →

finishing) a weft, the yarn ending by degrees, the ends being
brought out of the weaving between alternate warp ends.

Joining wefts should be achieved in a similar way – that is by the
overlapping and finishing of one, and the overlapping and beginning of the other, figure 6.2.

Darning in weft ends

All short ends left protruding from the weaving must eventually
be darned in. For this a 100 mm (4 in.) packing needle is required,
figure 6.3. Darning should follow the line of the *warp* either up
or down as shown in figure 6.4, and the ends finally trimmed off
flush with the surface of the rug. In the case of thicker yarns,
these can be separated into their constituent strands, and darned
into the same space, a little at a time.

6.3 *Left* 100 mm packing
needle

6.4 *Above* Darning in the
weft

Winding the shuttle

Figure 1.3, page 11, illustrates the method of winding yarn onto a
hand shuttle. The slip knot, tied at the end of the yarn, is passed
over the central peg of the shuttle. It then passes down round the
base to travel up the other side, once more passing round the peg.
Winding should continue in this way. Too much yarn on the
shuttle will result in yarns slipping from their correct positions, in
which case some of the yarn should be removed.

Weaving

Weaving should be carried out with the warp as taut as possible.
This will ensure that the weft threads beat-up against each other
more easily.

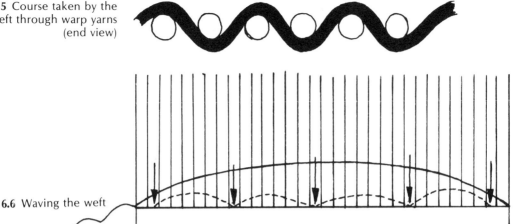

6.5 Course taken by the weft through warp yarns (end view)

6.6 Waving the weft

As the warp is usually a much harder yarn, it will be appreciated that when tensioned, it forms a rigid and inflexible series of threads through which the weft yarn has to pass. The weft yarn, being normally a much softer yarn and *unable to follow a straight course*, passes over and under the warp threads as it travels from one side of the weaving to the other. Figure 6.5 illustrates the course taken by the weft yarn. Because of this it is essential to provide enough slack in each pick. The process of introducing more yarn is called *waving* the weft. Figure 6.6 illustrates the method. This involves making an arc with the yarn in the open shed at each pick, which introduces the extra length required. Figure 6.6 indicates the way in which the yarn can be positioned in the shed to ensure equal spacing of the slack. This process is best done with the fingers, after which the batten (in the case of the loom) can be used to beat-up in the normal way. It is important to ensure that only sufficient slack is introduced to enable the yarn to follow comfortably round the hard threads of the warp. Excess slack will result in untidy loops occuring on the surface of the weaving. In the event of this happening the shed should be re-opened and the amount of yarn in the arc reduced.

Beating-up

When beating-up weft yarns, first *change the shed*. This will provide a more efficient and closer weave. Should the weft still fail to cover the warp properly, more slack may be needed. Sometimes a few more woven rows are all that is required.

Joining two woven pieces

Joining two pieces of weaving can be a simple operation providing certain precautions are taken.

The first of these is to ensure that the two pieces are as identical

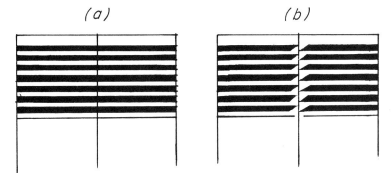

(a)   (b)

6.7 Designing a pattern suitable to accommodate a central join

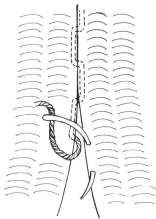

6.8 Stitching together two pieces of weaving

as it is possible to make them. This is best done by *counting each pick* and recording them on a plan or chart, rather than relying on measurement. When weaving the final strip or heading, add a few extra picks. These might be required when the two strips are finally sewn together. If it is found the extra is not required, it is a simple matter to unpick it and discard it.

If a flat woven technique is used, try to design a pattern which does not cross the join. Figure 6.7(a) illustrates the type of pattern to avoid. Here the horizontal strips are almost certain to get out of phase as weaving proceeds. A much better solution is shown in figure 6.7(b) where the join occurs in the area of the plain border. The same problem would not apply to a tufted rug where the joins would be completely disguised beneath the pile. Figure 6.8 illustrates the method of stitching two pieces of weaving together using a large curved needle. Darning should be carried out with the two pieces positioned correctly and secured (with heavy drawing pins) along the top heading to a flat surface. A bare wood floor is the best solution to this problem. Darning should commence at the top, working down. When the bottom heading is reached the extra weft yarns can be used to obtain a straight line across the weaving. The two pieces can then be finished off along the bottom fringe in the same way as the top. Darning should be carried out with the same yarn as used in the weft, ensuring that the thickness is sufficient to take the weight of the completed rug.

7 RYA OR LONG PILE WEAVING

This is one of the most popular of all rug weaving techniques and ideally suited to the beginner who has done little or no weaving.

There are two distinct elements in the Rya fabric, (i) a plain woven ground, which forms the rug itself, and (ii) rows of knots which are spaced at regular intervals and make the pile surface. The Rya technique originated in Scandinavia where it has been used for centuries for bed covers and wall hangings as well as rugs. It differs from the famous pile carpets of the East in the spacing of the knots and the length of the pile, but fundamentally they are both of the same construction. Figure 7.1 shows the Eastern carpet, with only two picks of plain weaving between the rows of knots and the short length of pile. In the Rya weave, the space between the rows is much larger, averaging eight to ten picks. The pile has to be long enough to cover this area and overlap the previous row by half of its length, so if the space between the rows is increased, the length of the pile is also increased. Figure 7.2 shows the difference between the Rya and the Eastern techniques. The Oriental rug has 6 mm ($\frac{1}{4}$ in.) tufts with 3 mm ($\frac{1}{8}$ in.) between the rows of knots, and the Rya has either 12 mm ($\frac{1}{2}$ in.) or 19 mm ($\frac{3}{4}$ in.) between the rows with a pile of 25 mm (1 in.) or 37 mm ($1\frac{1}{2}$ in.) respectively.

With its relatively high density of knots per unit area, the Oriental knotted carpet is slow and laborious to weave, and offers the designer the possibility of creating complex designs with fine detail. In contrast, Rya has a very low density of two or three knots to 25 mm (1 in.) weft-way and one row of knots every 15 mm - 50 mm ($\frac{3}{4}$ in. - 2 in.) warp-way, and gives great scope for a broader treatment of colour and texture. As the individual knots are usually made up of several strands of yarn, colours, fibres and texture can be blended with the utmost subtlety. A closely set Rya will show only the pile, so that the pattern in the pile is of major importance, but an open setting will show much of the ground, which can become the predominant factor in the design with the knots of pile arranged in isolated groups or blocks on the ground as well as in widely spaced straight lines. In Scandinavia, Rya rugs are often used upside down with the pile to the floor in the summer, when the shaggy warmth of the pile is not needed, and the smoother back creates a cooler effect. If this is to be done, the pattern of the ground must be as interesting as that of the pile.

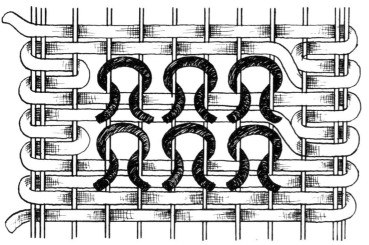

7.1 Close knotting – oriental rug

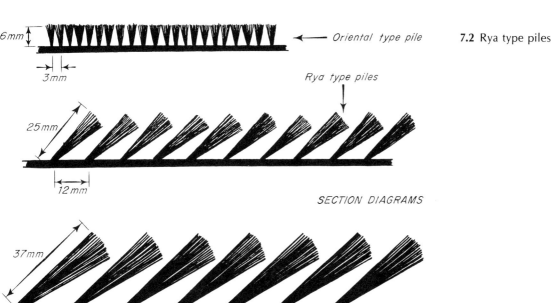

6 mm

Oriental type pile

7.2 Rya type piles

3 mm

Rya type piles

25 mm

12 mm

SECTION DIAGRAMS

37 mm

19 mm

A wide variety of materials can be used for Rya rugs. Though wool is the obvious first choice, cotton, linen, camel hair, and mohair are all suitable fibres for rugs, and even rags can be used with effect.

The woven samples

The samples illustrated in this chapter are woven in a combination of 6-ply and 2-ply carpet wool. The cotton warp is 16 double ends per 100 mm (4 double ends per inch). There are 8 knots per 100 mm (2 knots per inch), 19 mm (³/₄ in.) between the rows of knots and the pile is 37 mm (1½ in.) long.

6-ply rug yarn is used for the ground in a plain weave, and 6-ply and 2-ply are combined in the pile to vary the texture when only a few colours are used.

In samples where many colours are used, or a softer effect is required, 2-ply wool is used alone, as this offers better opportunities for colour mixing.

Each tuft is made up of a total of 24 individual strands of yarn, either 2 strands of 6-ply or 6 strands of 2-ply, giving 12 strands in the knot and therefore 24 strands in the complete tuft.

Approximate quantities for one square metre (yard)

6-ply rug wool for background weaving = 910 g (2 lb)
Cotton warp = 230 g (½ lb)
2-ply carpet wool for surface pile = 910 g (2 lb)

Colour mixing – equal quantities

The first sample (figure 7.3) is divided into three areas, two plain colours, and one a mixture of the two, creating a half-tone. 6-ply wool has been used in light orange and 2-ply in dark red/brown. In the central area, where the two colours were used together, mixing was done in the tuft. The alternative is to knot the colours alternately, but this is not successful in a small area.

7.3 *Below* Sample 1

7.4 *Right* Sample 2

Colour mixing – equal tones

In the second sample, figure 7.4, colours are used either side of a diagonal line. Both areas differ in tone but though the colours in each area vary from one another the tones of the colours in the whole square remain the same all over. From a short distance the effect of tone is more important than the effect of colour.

Considerable richness of colour can be achieved by blending in this way without destroying the shapes in the design, provided that the tonal values are maintained.

The 45° angle was made in a series of steps. One area was increased by two knots in each row while the other was similarly decreased.

Other angles can be made by various arrangements of steps, either shallow or steep, figure 7.5, and a combination of both can make a curved line.

Colour mixing – graduations

The third sample, figure 7.6, illustrates the final method of colour mixing, graduation. The combinations of six 2-ply yarns are

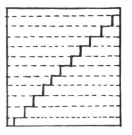

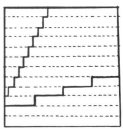

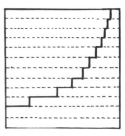

7.5 Creating angles by steps

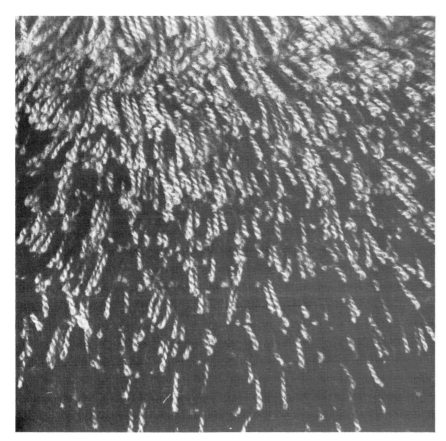

7.6 Sample 3

changed gradually over a series of twelve rows. The following table gives the composition of the knots in each row.

Row number	Dark strands	Light strands
1	6	0
2	5	1
3	5	1
4	4	2
5	4	2
6	3	3
7	3	3
8	2	4
9	2	4
10	1	5
11	1	5
12	0	6

Certain liberties may be taken with the strictly numerical sequence without detriment to the final effect, so that the sequence can be fitted into a given number of rows, as has been shown in the table. More than two colours can be used as shown in the following table.

Row number	Dark strands	Medium strands	Light strands
1			6
2		1	5
3		2	4
4		3	3
5		4	2
6		5	1
7	1	5	
8	2	4	
9	3	3	
10	4	2	
11	5	1	
12	6		

Designing for Ryas

There are many different ways of creating designs for weaving into Ryas. The methods suggested here have been chosen to illustrate some of them for the benefit of those just beginning. It is hoped that they will help to achieve satisfactory results right from the start.

Designing from the woven sample

For the experienced weaver the woven sample is always a prime source of inspiration. Most ideas can be tried within the confines

7.7 *Below* Design of twenty identical squares based on Sample 1

7.8 *Right* Design of twenty-four squares based on the same unit

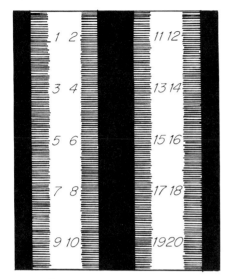

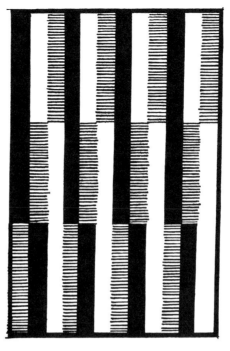

of a 300 mm (12 in.) or 350 mm (14 in.) warp without excessive waste of time or materials. Several samples may be necessary before a successful design is achieved, but once this has been done it is a relatively simple operation to repeat it on a larger scale.

The following diagrams show what can be done by assembling identical square units in different combinations. The squares were first drawn and painted and then cut out separately, and the many different patterns were created by arranging them in different ways. Using the first sample as an area of repeat, figure 7.7 shows a design achieved by the combination of twenty squares. The light and dark stripes are placed together to make larger areas of both tones. Figure 7.8 is a more complex arrangement of 24 squares in three groups of eight. The position of the three tones is changed in each group.

Using the diagonal idea in the second sample, figure 7.9 shows a design built up from twelve squares with the diagonals all running the same way, but with the tones reversed in some of the squares. Figure 7.10 uses an area of 24 squares and has diagonals running in both directions, as well as having the tones reversed in some of the squares. In this symmetrical design, the dark sides of the squares have been positioned as far as possible along the outer edges of the design.

Designs from Sample 3 have been constructed from graduated squares. The first uses graduated squares in both vertical and horizontal graduations, figure 7.11, and the second uses graduated squares in one direction only, figure 7.12.

7.9 *Top left* Design of 12 squares. Diagonals in one direction

7.10 *Above* Design of 24 squares. Diagonals in both directions

7.11 *Top centre* Design of 12 gradated square in two directions

7.12 *Top right* Design of 12 gradated squares in one direction

From these examples it will be seen how more squares can be added to create much larger areas of pattern. Figure 7.13 is an example of how a design can be built up to cover a much larger area, and how it can also be reduced to fit into a given rug size. Designs such as these can be treated in different ways. Altering the colouring plan can change the original design completely, and shapes can be added or taken out to assist in this process.

Designing on squared paper

As with all weaving, Ryas are to a certain extent conditioned by the vertical line of the warp and the horizontal line of the weft. Weaving takes place within this square grid so that one of the most logical ways of designing is on squared graph paper. This can be obtained in large sheets and a wide range of rulings, which can be chosen to match the proportions of the fabric to be designed. If the setting is one knot to the square centimetre (4 knots per square inch) a ruling as in figure 7.14(a) will provide the required proportion, and the sett will be 10 ends per 100 mm (4 single ends per inch). If longer tufts are required, the square unit is divided as in figure 7.14(b) into four rectangles, and the sett increased to 10 double ends per 100 mm (4 double ends per inch).

Before beginning the pattern, draw out the area representing the size of the finished rug. Lines on graph paper tend to be relatively light in tone, so that transparent colours are most suitable – Indian inks, watercolours, felt-tipped pens and coloured pencils are all excellent for this purpose. They can be used separately or mixed together. Squares can be coloured individually or combined to form shapes or stripes, and if larger areas of one colour are required, colouring squares with equal tones can provide a rich combination. All the patterns produced by these methods will be strongly geometric, figure 7.15.

7.13 *Opposite below right* Design of diagonal squares to cover larger area

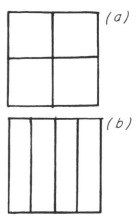

7.14 (a) and (b) Paper designing for Ryas – two grids

7.15 Design of coloured squares

Painted designs

Painting a design free of geometric restrictions is often preferred. Designs based on the textures of materials are usually better when freely designed. Squaring up the design is left until later.

There are many ways of attempting this kind of design. To take one example, instead of using paper in the normal way, paint on wet paper, crumpled paper or blotting paper. Each of these will give a different effect. Other methods involve the use of pulp paper, torn paper, and printing from paper. Many of these methods are described in the books *Design by Accident*, James O'Brian, Dover Publications, New York and *Creative Paper Craft* by Ernst Röttger, published by Batsford. Both provide ideas which can easily be adapted to make designs for rugs.

If the design will be spoiled by squaring it up, draw the square or rectangular grid with black ink on acetate or similar transparent film and lay this over the paper work.

7.16 Numerical diagram

Numerical diagrams

Numerical diagrams simplify the work of following the design during the weaving process. The yarns are dyed to correspond with the colours in the design and are then numbered. Squares or rectangles relating to the number of knots to the square centimetre (square inch) are drawn up on a chart, and the appropriate colour for each knot is marked on the diagram by its number, figure 7.16. Mixtures of colours will have several numbers. This diagram will supply all the information for weaving the rug, as the interpretation of the design has already been done, and much indecision during the making of the rug is avoided.

Warp yarn and setting for Ryas

The most generally useful setts for Rya rugs are:

16 single ends per 100 mm	4 single ends per inch – heavy yarn
24 single ends per 100 mm	6 single ends per inch – medium yarn
16 double ends per 100 mm	4 double ends per inch – fine yarn

Weaving the bottom edge

Using one 6-ply, or three 2-ply yarns wound together on the shuttle, weave about 50 mm (2 in.) in plain weave to ensure that there is sufficient to provide a border to the rug and a base on which the first row of tufts will lie. The amount of wool required for a rug is approximately 1.25 kg/m² (¼ lb/per sq ft), ie 375 gm for a 300 mm sample (¼ lb for a 12 in. sample), and 2.5 kg for a rug 1.25 m by 1.5 m (5 lb for a rug 48 in. x 60 in.).

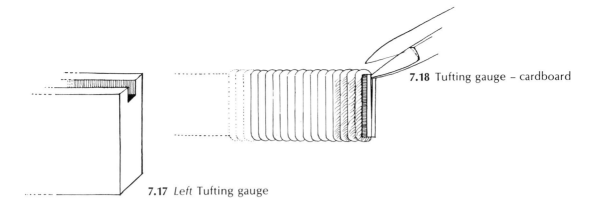

7.18 Tufting gauge – cardboard

7.17 *Left* Tufting gauge

Methods of knotting

There are various ways of knotting a pile rug, and the most generally useful is the Ghiordes knot, which is the one that most
weavers employ today. Knotting can be done from a continuous
thread or threads wound together, or from lengths cut to the
correct size prior to weaving. The choice is entirely personal, but
may be influenced by the design.

Knotting from a continuous thread means that yarns can be
taken up, grouped with other colours and discarded without prior
preparation. If, however, the weaver finds it more convenient to
cut lengths for the pile beforehand, the yarn should be cut on a
wooden gauge which can be made, or obtained from suppliers.
The usual gauge is a short length of wood with a groove cut along
one side, figure 7.17. The yarn is wound round the gauge, and
scissors or a knife blade inserted into the groove and the yarn
cut. Two pieces of card may equally well be used instead, the
blade of the scissors being inserted between the two pieces of
card and the yarn cut along one edge, figure 7.18. The total length
round the gauge must equal the length of both halves of the tuft
and an allowance for the knot itself. If 37 mm (1½ in.) tufts are
required it will be necessary to cut the yarn to a length of 90 mm
(3½ in.). The width of a card gauge should therefore be 45 mm
(1¾ in.).

With a continuous thread a guide rod is used. This method is
particularly useful when there is a continuous line of tufts of a
single colour, so the changes of colour are few. The yarn should
first be wound onto a small shuttle and the guide rod held in
position across the warp threads. The shuttle is passed round the
warp threads and the guide rod as shown in figure 7.19. The tufts
are then all cut in one process and the guide rod freed for the next
row. The length of the tufts is determined by the girth of the guide
rod. The rod has a groove down its length, and the tufts are cut
with a sharp knife running along the groove. Several rods of
different sizes will be needed for tufts of different lengths.

First row of knots
Leaving the two outside warp ends, start with ends 3 and 4, holding
them with the thumb and first finger of the left hand, while
making a knot as in figure 7.20 with the right. The weaving scissors
are held in the palm of the right hand with the third finger.

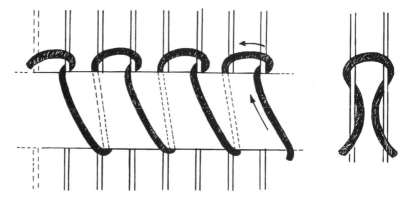

7.19 *Right* Knotting with a guide rod

7.20 *Far right* Ghourds knot

7.21 *Below* Weaving background level to top of knots at selvedge (one side)

7.22 *Below right* Weaving background level to top of knots at selvedge (other end of weaving)

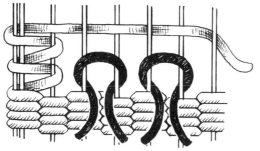 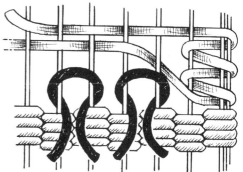

Repeat the process using threads 5 and 6, and continue across the warp, leaving the last two threads without a knot.

Weaving the selvedge

After completing a row of knots, take the shuttle with the ground weft and weave round the two selvedge threads until an amount equal to the depth of the row of knots has been completed, figure 7.21, which is four to six times. Having reached the level of the top of the knots, take the yarn through the next shed across the weaving to build up the other side in the same way, figure 7.22.

Continue plain weaving for eight to ten rows to weave about 20 mm (¾ in.) of ground and repeat the line of the tufts.

As the weaving and knotting proceed, the tufts will cover the background completely and half of the previous row of tufts and create the characteristic long pile surface. After completing the rug, finish off by weaving 50 mm (2 in.) of plain weave for the border and final edge.

8 TWISTED WEFT

Twisted weft is a simple technique used to create a number of small patterns in plain weave. Two 6-ply yarns are required, contrasting in tone, one light, one dark. This contrast is essential if the pattern effects created by the yarns are to be clearly seen. *Both yarns are wound onto one shuttle.*

The woven samples

The samples illustrate the weft-faced weave. Fine white cotton twine, threaded at 12 double threads to 100 mm (3 double threads per inch) constitutes the warp.

Sample 1 (figure 8.1) has been used to illustrate a number of controlled effects achieved by this process. 25 mm (1 in.) of plain weaving has been introduced between the sections to avoid confusion.

Section A All over spot
By twisting the central portion of alternate yarns into the reverse position in each shed an all-over spot effect is obtained. Figure 8.2 shows in detail the arrangement of the yarns.

Section B Horizontal lines
By reversing the order of colours in alternate rows, yarns of the same colour will come together to create a line, figure 8.3.

Section C Spot and line
By twisting the central portion of alternate yarns into the reverse position, an area of lines can be introduced into a background of spots. In this section, patterns A and B are combined. The rectangular shape is formed by changing the order of yarns at the same point each time, figure 8.4.

Section D Vertical stripes
The weft is twisted so that light and dark yarns cross each other on alternate warp threads, figure 8.5. In the second pick, the direction of twist is reversed. Pick one is then repeated. Vertical lines are created on two adjacent warp threads.

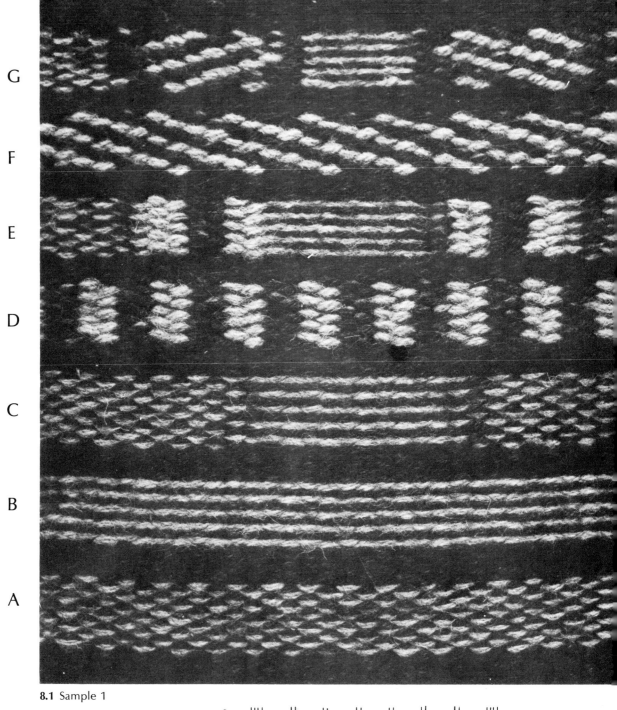

8.1 Sample 1

8.2 Section A All over spot

2nd Pick

3rd Pick

1st Pick

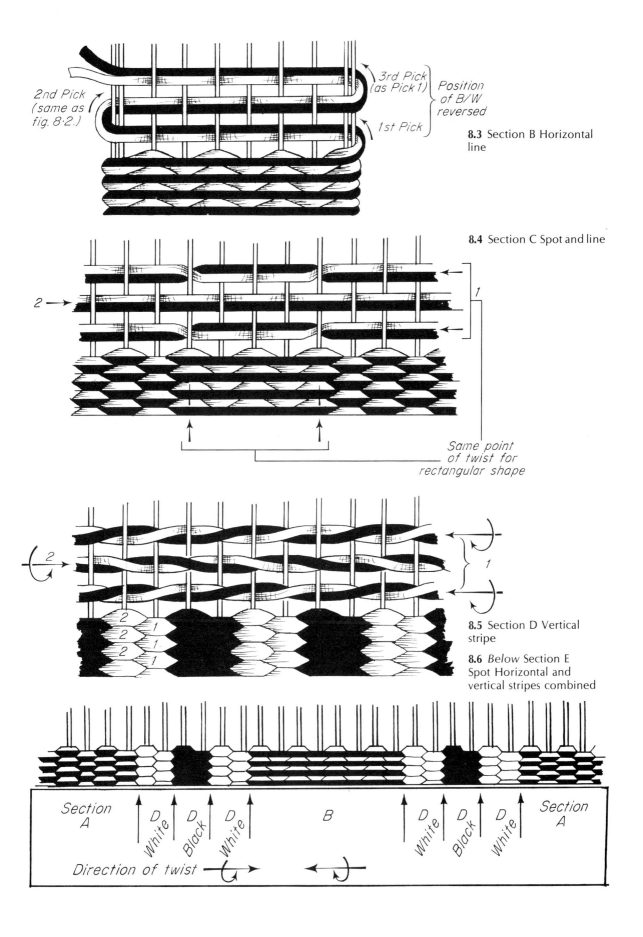

2nd Pick (same as fig. 8.2.)

3rd Pick (as Pick 1)
1st Pick
Position of B/W reversed

8.3 Section B Horizontal line

8.4 Section C Spot and line

2

1

Same point of twist for rectangular shape

2

1

8.5 Section D Vertical stripe

8.6 *Below* Section E Spot Horizontal and vertical stripes combined

Section A
D White
D Black
D White
B
D White
D Black
D White
Section A

Direction of twist

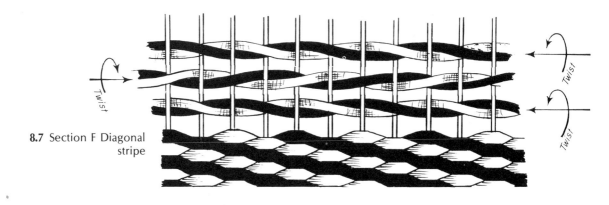

8.7 Section F Diagonal stripe

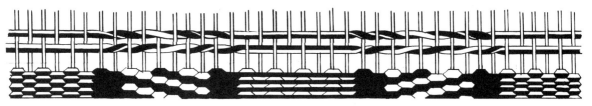

8.8 Section G Horizontal and vertical lines and diagonal combined

Section E Spot, horizontal and vertical stripe
Section E combines the patterns shown in A, B and D. In this section the vertical stripes are positioned as in D above. Working out combinations such as this on the loom is made easier if a diagram is first drawn out, showing the areas of pattern and the direction of twist of the yarn, figure 8.6.

Section F Diagonal stripe
Diagonal stripes are created in the same way as vertical stripes, by twisting the light and dark threads so that they cross each other on alternate warp threads, figure 8.7. The position of the crossing is moved one thread to the left or right, depending on the direction of the diagonal, on successive rows. In this pattern the direction of the twist remains constant, (clockwise for diagonal to the left and anti-clockwise for twill to the right). This means that the shuttle is twisted upwards going one way and downwards going the other to maintain a constant direction of twist.

Section G Combination of patterns
In this section all the above patterns are combined. The layout is symmetrical, the horizontal line occupying the central area, diagonals radiating on either side. The section terminates with the all-over spot at either edge. These three patterns are divided from each other by the dark section of the vertical stripe. Figure 8.8 shows the division of areas and the direction of twist of the yarns.

Sample 2 (figure 8.9) illustrates how other shapes can be used in the same way. Triangles, diamonds and wedge-like shapes can be made by following the instructions outlined above and at the same time moving the point at which the pattern changes in a series of steps to left or right.

72

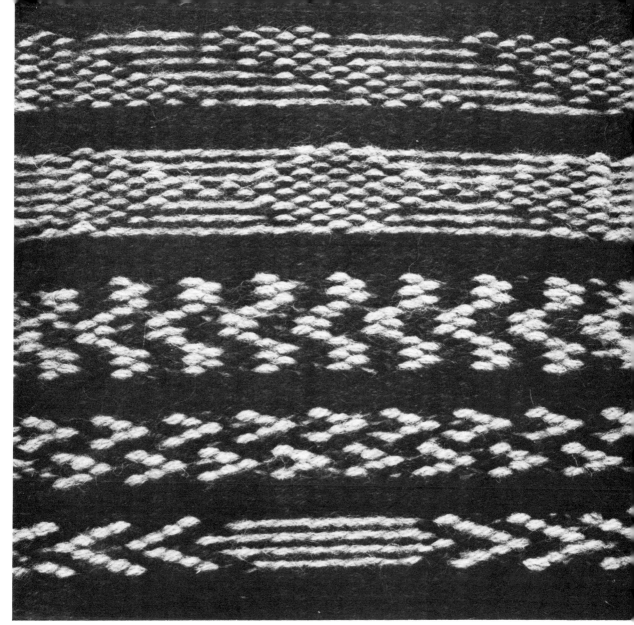

General design notes

8.9 Sample 2

There any many ways of developing rug designs from weaves of this type. These small-scale patterns can be achieved only by weaving. They cannot be drawn effectively on paper, so that ideas have to be worked out on the loom or weaving frame. Several samples may be required before all the problems of scale, proportion and colour have been solved.

In the following two samples an attempt has been made to illustrate how the design in Sample 4 was achieved from a small section of Sample 1. Section E was chosen, figure 8.6. Basically, there are two ways of developing this idea, (i) to continue the pattern as a vertical stripe and (ii) to include the areas of plain weave between the sections to create rectangular shapes. The

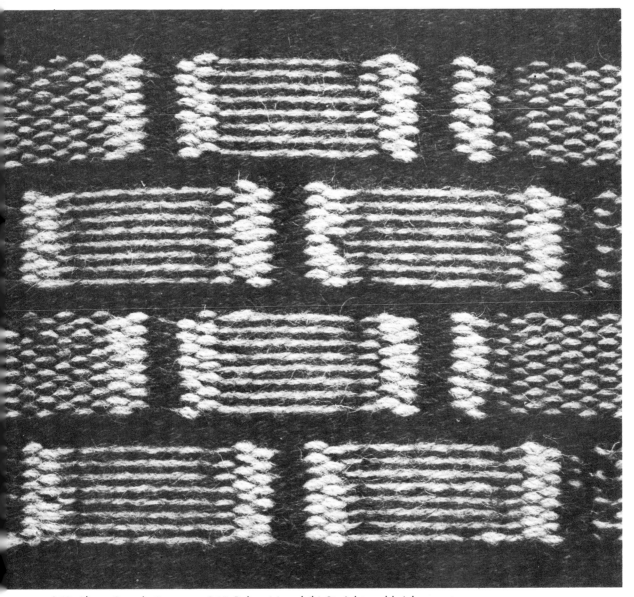

8.10 *Above* Sample 3   **8.11** *Below* (a) and (b) Straight and brick repeats

(a)

(b)

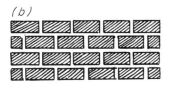

latter arrangement was chosen, and samples 3 and 4 illustrate the development of the idea. Sample 3 (figure 8.10) shows how the size of the patterned rectangles was first enlarged to twice their height, and the arrangement of the repeat decided. Here two alternatives were possible, a straight repeat, figure 8.11(a), or a half-drop or 'brick' repeat, figure 8.11(b), the latter being chosen. In sample 4 (figure 8.12) several more changes were made. The size of the rectangles was again increased, this time to twice their length, and the patterns woven to alternate in groups of one and two, figure 8.13(b), instead of one and one, figure 8.13(a).

8.12 Sample 4

8.13 *Below* (a) and (b) Brick repeats 2/1 and 1/3

Finally, to provide a variation of colour over the length of the design, a gradation of yellows was introduced, so that each successive row of rectangles changes colour from primrose to deep gold. Over an even larger area it might be necessary to repeat the same colour for several rows so that the graduation was more gradual, but again, this would have to be tried so that the effect could be seen before a final decision could be made. The background colour remains the same throughout, as does the width of the plain weaving between the rows. These are woven to correspond to the area between the shapes and so provide a balanced ground.

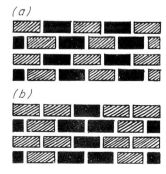

(a)

(b)

9 TWO, THREE OR FOUR SHUTTLE TECHNIQUES

The woven samples

All the samples illustrating this chapter have been woven in treble 2-ply carpet yarn on a fine cotton twine warp, 16 double ends per 100 mm (4 double ends per inch). The weave is plain weave.

Samples 1 and 2 use two shuttles only, one with light pink yarn and the other with dark brown.

In the first sample (figure 9.1) the three basic woven patterns are shown. These are made by using the two shuttles in different sequences as follows:

9.1 Sample 1

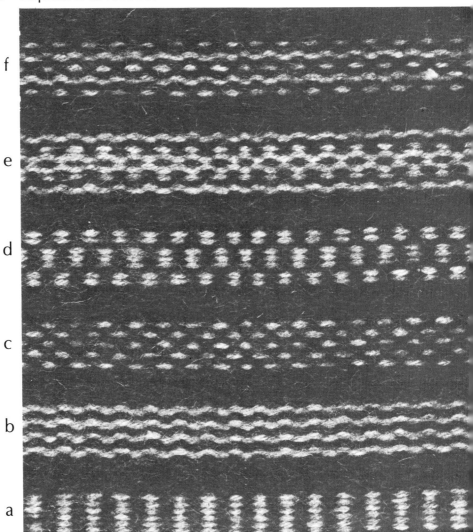

f

e

d

c

b

a

(a) *Warp stripe: 1 and 1 wefting*
This pattern has the appearance of a vertical line. It is obtained by using the two shuttles alternately in consecutive sheds, one pick light, one pick dark.

(b) *Weft stripe: 2 and 2 wefting*
This has the appearance of a thin wavy horizontal line and is obtained by weaving two picks successively of the same colour, one in each shed.

(c) *All-over spot: 1 and 2 wefting*
This is obtained by the third sequence of wefting, one pick of the first colour followed by two successive picks of the second colour in the two succeeding sheds.

In the next three bands on sample 1, ie (d), (e) and (f), simple patterns have been made by using (a), (b) and (c) in different ways. These patterns also show the device of mirror repeats, which double the width of a narrow stripe by repeating the colouring plan of the stripe in the reverse order. Band (f) has the spot as the basis of the design, (e) the weft stripe and (d) the warp stripe. These patterns may appear complicated to the weaver with little experience, but, by weaving samples, the way that the designs are constructed will soon become apparent.

Samples 2, 3 and 4 illustrate a method of expanding a two-shuttle, two colour design into designs using three or four shuttles and colours, Samples 3 and 4 respectively. For a simple explanation of this process, Sample 2 (colour plate 1 facing page 96) can be seen to be divided into three basic areas: first– light, where the pink yarn is woven alone; second– half-tone, where the pink and brown yarns are combined in the pattern sequence; third– dark, where the brown is woven alone. To increase the number of colours, the patterned sequences are introduced into the light and dark areas using yarns similar in tone, though not necessarily similar in colour.

In Sample 3, (colour plate 1 facing page 96) the light areas (pink) have been patterned by the introduction of a second colour – lilac. As this colour is similar in tone, the general effect of a light area is retained.

Finally, Sample 4 (colour plate 1 facing page 96) shows the introduction of a dark red yarn into the dark brown areas. In this way a four shuttle, four colour design is achieved.

Sample 5 (colour plate 1 facing page 96) shows an alternative method of introducing four or more colours. In this sample the colours are mixed by degrees in the shuttle. The basic pattern remains the same as in Sample 2, and two shuttles only are used. Figure 9.2 illustrates the method of mixing colours. These gradate from plain dark brown at the border to light yarns in the centre and back again.

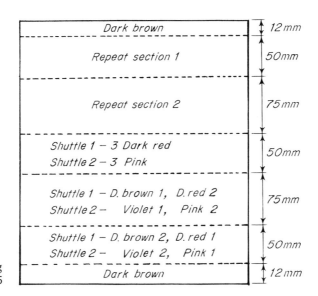

Dark brown	12 mm
Repeat section 1	50mm
Repeat section 2	75 mm
Shuttle 1 – 3 Dark red Shuttle 2 – 3 Pink	50mm
Shuttle 1 – D. brown 1, D. red 2 Shuttle 2 – Violet 1, Pink 2	75mm
Shuttle 1 – D. brown 2, D. red 1 Shuttle 2 – Violet 2, Pink 1	50mm
Dark brown	12 mm

9.2 Diagram illustrating colours used in Sample 5

All these samples have an area of pattern about 300 mm (12 in.) square. For a full-sized rug this area can either be repeated to the length required, or thought of as a complete rug on a small scale. If the latter is considered, it is essential that the various areas of light, dark and half-tone be retained in the same proportion. This can be achieved only by elongating the sample equally over its entire length. To achieve this effect, repeat each 25 mm (1 in.) of the sample 4 or 5 times, depending on the length required.

Two shuttle weaves

Before starting to weave, select two contrasting colours, one for each shuttle, in 6-ply or treble 2-ply carpet yarn.

Although fundamentally this is a simple technique, it has complications. It is difficult to achieve a perfect selvedge. A simple method sometimes used is for all yarns weaving the pattern to pass round the selvedge threads, even though this may mean passing over or under two warp threads in the process. This method is far from satisfactory, especially where colours are not weaving consecutively, and where one colour may be discontinued, only to be introduced again a few rows later.

The following notes describe some solutions to these problems. A perfect selvedge can be achieved in which the pattern is continued to the very edge of the weave. It is shown how all the yarns can be carried forward, even though they may not be weaving at the time. This system is a little difficult to grasp to begin with, but with a little experience the process becomes automatic and the effort is well worth while. The diagrams illustrate the methods used in each of the three sequences. The weaving is shown 'opened out', whereas the patterns are effective only when the rows of weft have been beaten down into place.

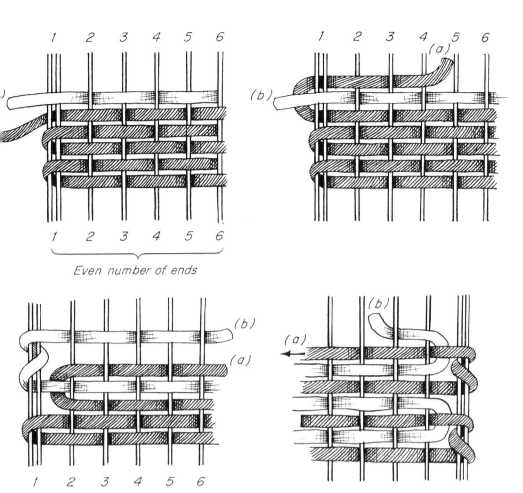

1 2 3 4 5 6

Even number of ends

1 2 3 4 5 6

The weaves

1 Warp stripes or pick and pick stripes

Description for weaving with an *even* number of warp ends.

Weave 37 mm (1½ in.) in plain weave with the darkest colour yarn (a) to provide a border to the design, finishing at the left hand side of the sample. Introduce a second colour (b) at the opposite side and weave one pick across. This will bring both yarns to the left hand side of the sample, one yarn (b) above and one (a) below the selvedge thread, figure 9.3. Pass yarn (a) straight back into the next shed, ignoring the selvedge threads altogether. It will be prevented from running back by yarn (b), figure 9.4. Yarn (b) should now pass under and up, circling the selvedge thread once to fill the gap left by (a), figure 9.5, before entering the next shed.

On the other edge of the sample the yarns will be in the reverse order, ie yarn (b) which was over the selvedge thread on the previous side, will now be underneath. A similar procedure should be adopted on this side, the only difference being that yarn (a) will *first* circle the outside thread, under and over, whilst (b) will enter the next shed after this operation, figure 9.6. Continue to repeat

9.3 *Top left* Pick and pick (1-1) warp stripes on even number ends 2 shuttles. First position of yarns

9.4 *Top right* Pick and pick (1-1) warp stripes on even number ends 2 shuttles. Second position of yarns

9.5 *Bottom left* Pick and pick (1-1) warp stripes on even number ends 2 shuttles. Third position of yarns

9.6 *Bottom right* Pick and pick (1-1) warp stripes on even number ends 2 shuttles. Fourth position of yarns

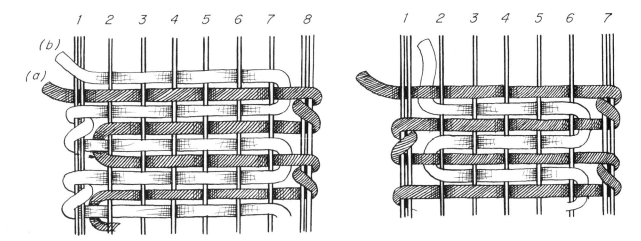

9.7 Complete view

9.8 *Right* Pick and pick (1-1) weaving on odd number warp ends 2 shuttles

these two rows. Figure 9.7 shows the whole operation for an even number of warp ends, and figure 9.8 shows the procedure for an odd number of warp ends.

2 Weft stripes for two and two picks

Description of weaving with an even number of warp ends.

For this pattern the selvedge sequence is more simple, as each shuttle will be weaving an even number of rows, and the weft yarns will automatically pass round the selvedge thread each time. In so doing it must also circle the other yarn, figure 9.9. This operation will carry each yarn forward for the following shed in a logical sequence, figure 9.10. On the other edge of the sample the same procedure is adopted, figure 9.11, the yarns lying in the alternative position.

Obviously, horizontal stripes can be widened by increasing the number of picks, eg 3 and 3, 4 and 4, etc.

9.9 *Below* Weft Stripes (2-2 picks) on even ends 2 shuttles

9.10 *Below right* Weft Stripes (2-2 picks) on even warp ends 2 shuttles. Second position

Increasing with an even number of rows is straightforward. As with 2 and 2 stripes, the weft yarn not being used is carried up at the selvedge, the weaving yarn encircling it each time before entering the following shed. Figure 9.12 shows the process with groups of four rows.

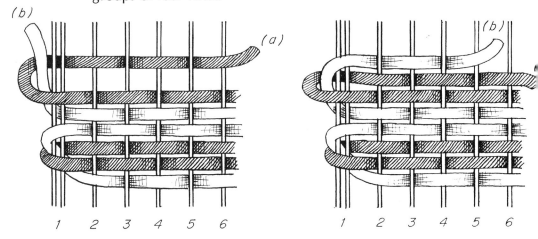

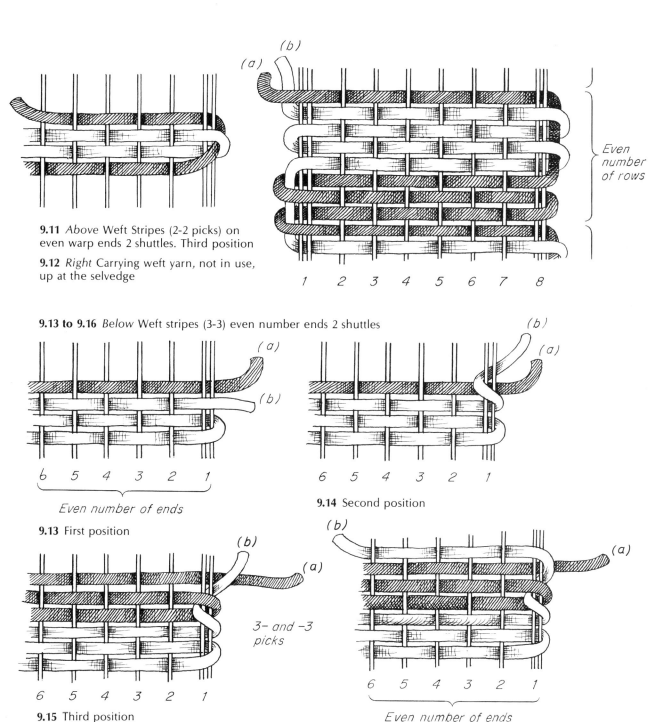

9.11 *Above* Weft Stripes (2-2 picks) on even warp ends 2 shuttles. Third position

9.12 *Right* Carrying weft yarn, not in use, up at the selvedge

Even number of rows

1   2   3   4   5   6   7   8

9.13 to 9.16 *Below* Weft stripes (3-3) even number ends 2 shuttles

6   5   4   3   2   1

Even number of ends

9.13 First position

9.14 Second position

6   5   4   3   2   1

3- and -3 picks

6   5   4   3   2   1

9.15 Third position

6   5   4   3   2   1

Even number of ends

9.16 Fourth position

 When an odd number of picks is required, eg 3 and 3, it will be necessary to make a slight adjustment at the selvedge. In figure 9.13, the yarn (b) is lying over the selvedge thread at the end of its row. Pass it under and over the selvedge, figure 9.14, before circling it with yarn (a). Yarn (a) will then weave its three rows, figure 9.15, and yarn (b) will be in the correct position to enter the next shed, figure 9.16, for weaving the following three rows.

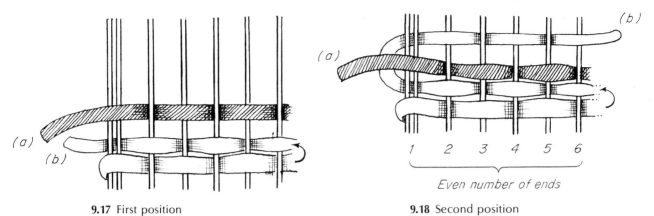

9.17 First position

9.18 Second position

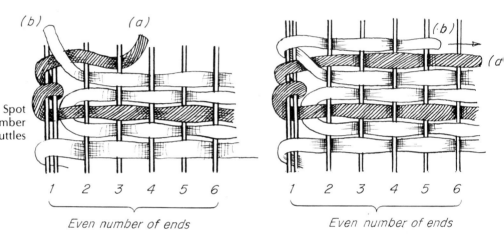

9.17 to 9.20 All Over Spot (1-2 picks) even number ends 2 shuttles

Even number of ends

9.19 Third position

Even number of ends

9.20 Fourth position

9.21 *Below* Complete procedure

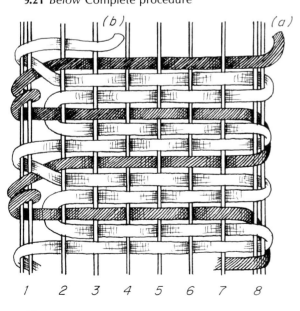

9.22 Warp spot (1-3 picks) even number ends 2 shuttles plain weave

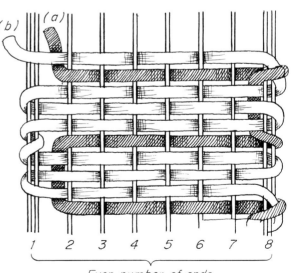

Even number of ends

3 All-over spot – one and two picks

Descriptions for weaving with an even number of warp ends.

After weaving two rows of yarn (b), weave one pick only of yarn (a). This will bring the yarns to the same side of the weaving, one yarn on each side of the selvedge thread, figure 9.17. Now follow the sequence as for pick and pick warp stripes, that is (b) will pass straight back into the next shed, figure 9.18, and weave two picks, while (a) will be wrapped round the selvedge by going *under* it first and then circling it in an upward direction before entering the next shed, figure 9.19. Yarn (b) will then also pass under and round the selvedge thread before entering the next shed in a cross-like movement, figure 9.20, making the woven edge firm with the threads fitting together. At the other side of the weaving, the two yarns circle the selvedge thread each time. Figure 9.21 illustrates the whole process.

This system is identical for an odd or an even number of ends. Other spot effects are obtained by weaving more than two picks of yarn (b). By using a sequence of 1 and 3, a similar effect will be obtained, but more openly spaced.

Figure 9.22 shows the whole operation for an even number of warp ends, and figure 9.23 shows the procedure for an odd number of warp ends. There is a great similarity between these methods and the warp stripe 1 and 1 sequence already described.

9.23 Warp spot (1-3 picks) odd number ends 2 shuttles plain weave

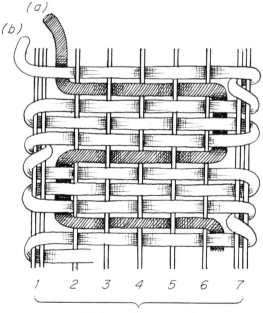

(a)

(b)

1   2   3   4   5   6   7

Odd number of ends

10 TIE & DYE & DIP-DYE WEFTS

Weft yarns dyed by these methods produce unusual and often unexpected results. Instead of being of one colour, the yarn is part-dyed in several colours, so that a multi-coloured yarn is produced. Plain weave only is used, and the pattern develops as the weaving progresses, according to the patches of colour on the yarn.

Tie and dye is now well known, although its use in this context may be less familiar. The technique is one of resist dyeing, for by knotting the hank of yarn tightly with itself, or by wrapping waste thread tightly round the hank in some parts only, the colour of the dyebath is prevented from reaching the covered parts of the yarn. Dip-dyeing is a more restricted method. In this case the hank is not wrapped, but suspended above the dyebath, so that only those parts to be dyed enter the water. Dip-dye and tie and dye offer unique opportunities for cross-dyeing effects where one colour, for example yellow, crosses, ie is dyed on top of another colour, blue, to produce a third colour, green.

In many of the samples woven to illustrate this chapter, only three colours were used, yellow, magenta, and blue. These three hues provide the three essential tones required for successful colour mixing, light (yellow), medium (magenta) and dark (blue). Using these three in various depths of tone and sequence is an effective formula for anyone cross-dyeing for the first time. For the more experienced weaver, however, it is rather limiting, and he will find it better to separate the available colours into the three tonal categories and select one colour from each group. Dyeing is best carried out using each colour separately, with the minimum of mixing of the colours in the dyebath. This contributes enormously to the richness and brilliance of the final colours, however dark they may be. Cross-dyeing subtle and unusual colours all too often results in gloomy and muddy tones.

One of the main advantages of tie and dye is that comparatively small dyebaths can be used for quite large quantities. This is due to the fact that when much of the wool has been closely knotted or wrapped to resist the dye, much less space is required. The main disadvantage of these methods is that on the whole they are diffi-cult to regulate, and chance plays an important part in the final result. In addition, these accidental effects are difficult to repeat if required.

The weaver must be prepared to improvise, and not have too rigid an idea when starting out. Often failures can be turned into successes by tying and dyeing again, and frequently a most unpromising yarn will weave up into fascinating patterns.

The woven samples

All the samples were woven in Paton's 6-ply Turkey rug wool on a warp of fine cotton netting twine at 16 double ends in 100 mm (4 double ends per inch). ICI Coomasse acid dyes were used throughout, following the commercial dyeing instructions. Approximately 250 g (½ lb) of wool was used for each sample.

Random patterns – single-colour dyeing

Sample 1 (colour plate 2 facing page 97) illustrates the effect obtained from the most simple of the resist methods – knotting the hank. In this case the wool was already dyed, and the hanks were knotted in two places, figure 10.1. After preliminary wetting they were placed in the dyebath until the required depth of tone was reached. After rinsing they were untied, dried, and woven in plain weft-faced weave. It will be seen that where the knots occur, patches of yarn remain undyed. These make the pattern of spots which occur at random on the sample.

10.1 Knotting the hank

Random patterns – multi-coloured dyeing

In Sample 2 (colour plate 2 facing page 97) the same method was followed, except that the hanks were knotted and dyed three times. The lightest colour (yellow) was used first, and after dyeing the hanks were rinsed, untied and retied *over the coloured portions*. In this way as much as possible of the preceding colour was protected from the following colour. This procedure was repeated again for the third and final colour, blue.

Methods of controlling tie and dye patterns start by relating the length of the hank to the width of the warp. Even so, the pattern is sometimes subject to the whim of the yarn. Sample 3 (colour plate 2 facing page 97) is a design produced by this method.

Beginning with the design roughs carried out on small scale graph paper, patterns were restricted to simple rectangular shapes

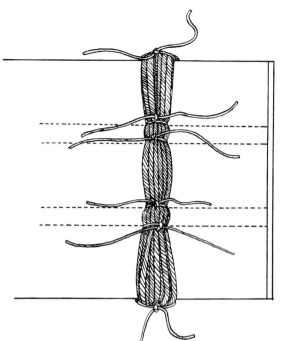

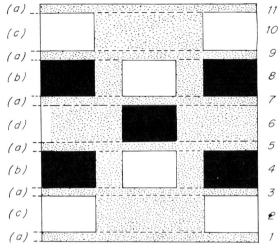

(a)		11
(c)		10
(a)		9
(b)		8
(a)		7
(d)		6
(a)		5
(b)		4
(a)		3
(c)		2
(a)		1

10.2 Winding hank on card for tie and dye

10.3 *Right* Diagram showing the eleven sections of Sample 3

and stripes. Coloured felt pens were used to provide the cross-dyeing effects.

Having decided on the layout of shapes and colours, the design was enlarged for a 300 mm (12 in.) sample by using proportionately larger graph paper.

The original hanks were re-wound onto a piece of heavy card 350 mm (14 in.) across (the additional 50 mm (2 in.) being for take-up and shrinkage), to measure the length of the hank. The card was also drawn up with lines to indicate the width of the shapes, figure 10.2.

The card must be sufficiently long for all the yarn to be wound on to it without overlapping, and the tension must be even and not too tight. When sufficient yarn has been wound, the end should be tied to the thread next to it on the edge of the card.

The designs are based on a weft density of 8 picks per centimetre (18 picks per inch). Figure 10.3 shows how the pattern was divided into eleven sections, five sections of 30 picks, six sections of eight. The repetitive nature of the design allowed for the winding of the hanks to be done in three groups. One complete hank was wound for the plain sections (a) consisting of 48 picks in all (50 wound), four hanks of sections (b) and (c) consisting of 30 picks each (34 wound) and one hank of section (d) consisting of 30 picks (34 wound).

To provide a rich mottled effect of all colours, the wool was first knotted on its original hanks and dyed yellow. After washing and drying, these hanks were wound into balls ready for winding onto the card. The five sections (b), (c) and (d) were wound separately. Loops were tied round the hanks on both edges. These loops (top and bottom), if tightly knotted, will produce a thin line on the yarn during dyeing, which indicates the exact point during weaving at which the yarn turns at the selvedge to enter the

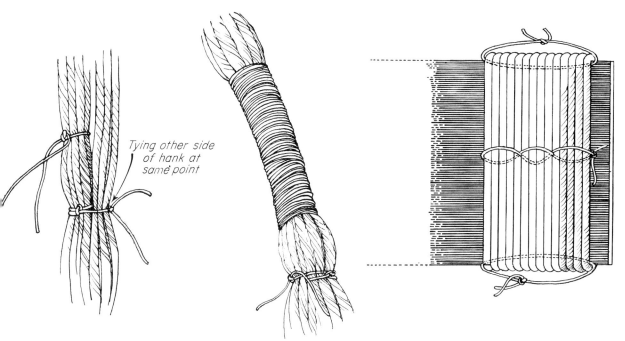

Tying other side of hank at same point

next shed. This enables the weaver to decide whether or not to add or remove one or more of the outside warp threads to obtain the correct width and alignment of the pattern before starting to weave. Additional loops were tied to indicate the edges of the shapes as shown by the lines on the card. Each loop was left with long ends so that after removing the hank from the card the other side of the hank could be tied at the same point, figure 10.4.

All the hanks were then dyed light pink, the lightest colour of the design. After washing the hanks and spinning dry, the areas between the loops that were intended to remain light were bound tightly with a mercerised linen yarn, figure 10.5. (Shiny cotton string is also excellent for this purpose.) All the hanks were then dyed a deep orange/brown.

After dyeing the hanks, washing and spinning dry, the areas that were intended to remain orange/brown were bound, including the hanks for section (a), and dyed in a strong solution of blue. Tying for the final colour was not done with the exactness of the previous colours, as flecks of dark were required to occur at random over the areas of orange to add richness and variety to the surface texture.

Controlled patterns – dip-dye

As with tie and dye controlled patterns, controlling dip-dye patterns starts by relating the length of the hank to the width of the warp. For Sample 4 (colour plate 2 facing page 97), which measures 300 mm (12 in.) across, the original hanks were re-wound onto pieces of card 350 mm (14 in.) across. Again the card must be sufficiently long for all the yarn to be wound on to it without overlapping, and the tension must be even and not too tight. When sufficient yarn has been wound, the end should be tied to the

10.4 *Left* Tying other side of hank at same point

10.5 *Centre* Binding hank with twine to resist dye

10.6 *Above* Winding hank on card for dip-dye

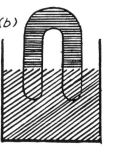

(a)

(b) (c)

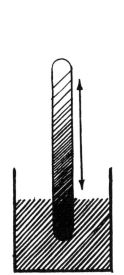

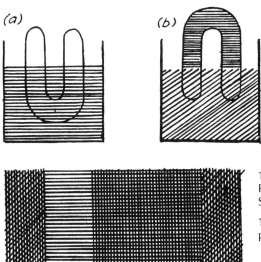

10.7 *Above* (a), (b) and (c) Positions of dip-dye hank for Sample 4

10.9 *Left* Diagrams showing position of tones in Sample 4

10.8 *Above* Gradating tones, dip-dye

thread next to it on the edge of the card. Before removing the hank from the card it should be tied with a loose figure-of-eight knot on either side, figure 10.6, and in addition a loop should be tied at each end for use in the dyeing process. (Mercerised cotton or linen twine is advised).

The amount of yarn required for weaving can be calculated by counting the number of picks to the centimetre (inch) in a similar piece of weaving. With a 6-ply rug yarn of the type used for these samples, there are 72 picks to the 100 mm (18 picks per inch). Figure 10.7 illustrates the dyeing procedure used to obtain Sample 4 (colour plate 2 facing page 97). As this design required the identical use of colour for both yellow and magenta, the ends of the hank were bent round and dipped in the dye to the same level. Dyeing blue was the exception, and this produced the final off-centre arrangement of the light stripe. Hanks can be suspended from rods resting on the sides of the dyebath, the level of the liquid being adjusted to give the required amount of colour on the hank. In some cases it may be necessary to hold the hank at the correct height by hand until sufficient dye has been absorbed.

Obviously there are many alternative ways of dip-dyeing hanks, and unlimited variations in designing the positions and sizes of the areas of colour, and the cross-dyed areas. It is also worth remembering that gradations of colour can be achieved by keeping the yarn constantly on the move in the dyebath, figure 10.8.

When weaving begins it is essential that the yarns be arranged in their correct position according to the design, otherwise quite different results will occur. Pick and pick (1 and 1) effects can be produced by positioning the yarn at random in the shed, and diagonals by weaving on a warp not precisely matched to the length of the hank. Warps either slightly wider or narrower will produce this effect, the pattern gradually shifting diagonally across the weaving as in Sample 5 (colour plate 2 facing page 97).

10.10 *Opposite* Sample 7

Weaving full-sized rugs from the samples will necessarily require additional organisation, and decisions will have to be made concerning scale and repeats. On the whole it is a good idea to treat the sample as the complete rug design in tie and dye, simply enlarging it to the required size, while retaining the proportions. Full-sized rugs can present problems with this technique, in that often much time is required tying the yarn prior to dyeing. Some weavers use other methods such as threading the yarn through bicycle inner tubing and tying each end tightly to resist the entry of the dye. This method, though efficient, precludes the opportunities for mottled effects, and a simple solution is to group together the yarns for identical sections in the design and warp them as one hank. Hanks can also be folded onto themselves, when the pattern allows, and wrapped in the same way. These methods reduce considerably the time required to warp large amounts of wool, and also the quantity of thread required.

There are many other ways in which tie and dye methods can be applied to other rug weaving techniques, and the final samples in this section illustrate some of the possibilities.

Sample 6 (colour plate 2 facing page 97) shows the use of tie and dye in a warp-faced weave. Details relating to the construction of rugs of this type are to be found in chapter 13. Tie and dye warps are well known in Eastern European countries, India and other parts of the world, where they have for centuries been used for patterning finely-woven cloths. This technique is known as Ichatt of Ikat.

Sample 7 (figure 10.10) shows the use of tie and dye in a Rya long pile technique. In this sample the yarns for the tufts were cut beforehand to the required length and tied so that just the tips of the tufts retained their original colour, the remainder being dyed black. Black 6-ply rug yarn was also used for the plain woven ground.

11 KHELIM OR SLIT TAPESTRY

Khelim or slit tapestry is a weft-faced plain weave ideally suited to the limitations of a weaving frame or a simple two-shaft loom.

History

Fragments of cloth woven in this technique have been discovered in many parts of the world, some dating back to the third millenium BC. As with the knotted carpet technique, this technique has flourished mainly in the Middle East, Asia Minor and India, and it is from these areas that some of the finest examples have come. It would seem that Khelim, derived from the Arabic word for curtain, was first woven as a hanging or a wall-covering, but whatever its origin, the technique produced strong decorative fabrics ideally suited to the practical needs of a nomadic life. Items including saddle-bags, horse trappings, blankets, bed covers and narrow strips for tying-up goods were all woven by this method.

Technique

The distinguishing feature of this technique is that the yarns are used in relatively short lengths, each weaving its own small geometric shape. Unless a plain area is required, yarns do not run continuously from selvedge to selvedge as in the weaving methods so far considered. Instead, there may be a dozen or more separate yarns weaving across the warp, each keeping to a limited number of warp ends.

Weaving is carried out with the yarns wound into finger hanks. These are made by winding the yarn round the thumbs and little finger of one hand in a figure-of-eight loop, figure 11.1(a). After completing eight to ten loops, the yarn is removed from the hand and winding is continued around the loops, figure 11.1(b), until sufficient yarn has been wound, figure 11.1(c). These hanks are passed through the shed in a vertical position and can be pushed between the threads of the warp to rest on the weaving when not in use.

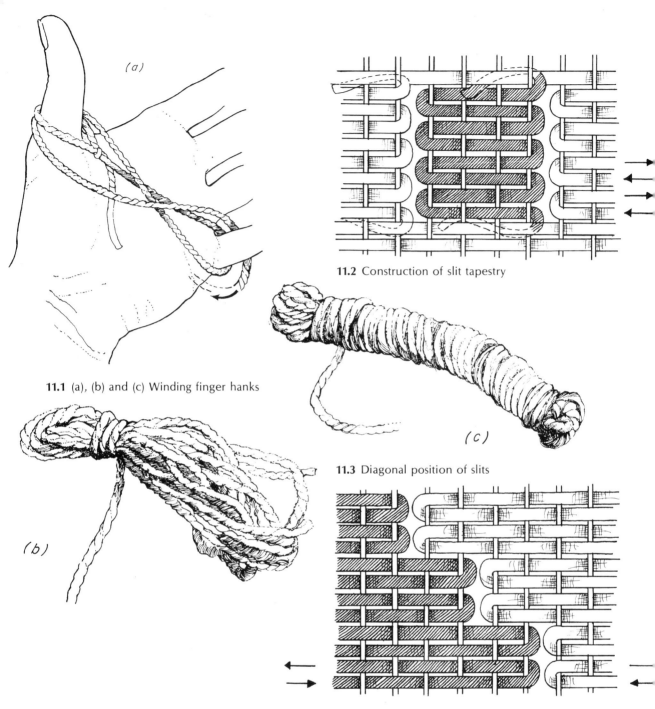

11.1 (a), (b) and (c) Winding finger hanks

11.2 Construction of slit tapestry

11.3 Diagonal position of slits

Construction

Figure 11.2 illustrates the way in which Khelim is constructed. The two adjoining shapes are woven independently of each other, each weft yarn working backwards and forwards only through its own group of warp threads till the small block is completed. This results in vertical slits between every pair of blocks, and means that the weaving is held together only by the yarns weaving across above and below the slit.

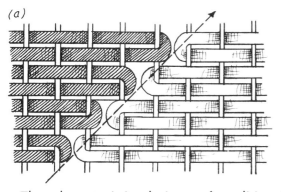

(a)

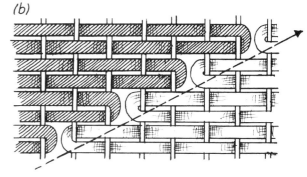

(b)

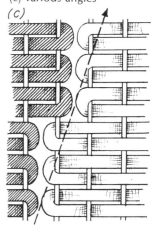

11.4 (a), 45° Angle (b) and (c) various angles

(c)

The characteristic designs of traditional Khelims are indicative of the way in which the patterns evolved from the technique, as the slits had to be staggered across the width of the weaving, figure 11.3. The result is a pattern with a strong accent on the diagonal. Weavers of classical Khelims achieved a rich variety of zigzag designs and motifs built up of triangular, diamond and related shapes.

For this type of pattern the lines would run normally at an angle of 45°, and this can be achieved by stepping regularly across the weaving with steps in which the height and width are similar, figure 11.4(a). By varying the number of picks in the height of a step, or the number of warp threads in the width of a step, it is possible to construct many different angles, figure 11.4(b) and (c). By a combination of deep and shallow steps it is possible to weave a circle, figure 11.5.

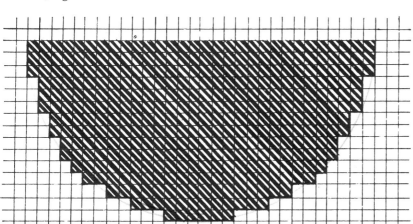

11.5 Half circle

Colour

Khelim offers opportunities for the use of an unlimited number of colours. Shapes can be woven in either one colour only, or in a combination of colours. These can be either mixed beforehand in the finger hank or laid in the shed in short lengths at random. It is also possible for patterns such as those which are described in chapter 9 *Two, three and four shuttle techniques*, to be woven in this way, although it would be necessary to ensure that the shapes being woven were large enough to take the additional pattern. Normally the number of colours required depends on the design being woven and the number of shapes that it contains.

Some readers may feel insufficiently skilled in the use of colour to attempt a design involving a colour scheme beyond the range of the three or four colours normally required. The outlines given in chapter 9 may help in this context, and some additional suggestions here may help those who would hesitate before starting designs of this type. The samples illustrating this chapter have been specially designed to make the weaving of khelims easily understood. In this, colour plays an important part and the samples themselves not only develop technically but also in the way that the colours are used.

A range of Welsh woollen yarns in seven natural colours was used throughout the samples. They can be obtained from the suppliers in a sequence of tones ranging from white to dark brown, and include three mixtures or marl yarns. In the first two samples the yarns were used in their natural state, but in Samples 3 and 4, yarns were dyed in a solution of yellow and light orange respectively.

The advantage of this method is that without too much difficulty a range of closely related colours is produced, which can be used confidently, knowing that all the colours will blend together successfully to give the design a strong sense of colour unity. It must be appreciated, however, that this methods works well only when comparatively light colours are used. The darker the dye-bath the more limited the tonal range.

The main disadvantage in weaving Khelim is that it is slow to weave, but the speed will naturally be influenced by the complexity of the design. In Samples 1, 2 and 3, areas of plain weave were introduced between groups of small shapes. This not only helped to simplify the general design but also to speed up the weaving process.

The woven samples

Sample 1 Exercise in maximum slit
A simple exercise with which to start weaving Khelim is to design and weave a pattern in which the vertical slit is used to its maximum length.

Sample 1, figure 11.6, is an example of this design with slits measuring 30 mm (1¼ in.) long. It is advisable not to go beyond this measurement if the weaving is to remain practical as a floor covering and not become a hazard to walking. The length of the slit could be increased considerably, however, if the weaving were designed for some other purpose, for a wall-covering or a bed-cover, for example.

Before weaving this sample the position of the slits and their

11.6 Sample 1

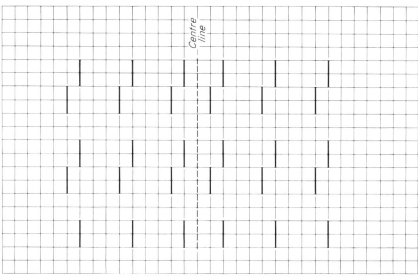

Centre line

11.7 Layout of slits
(Sample 1)

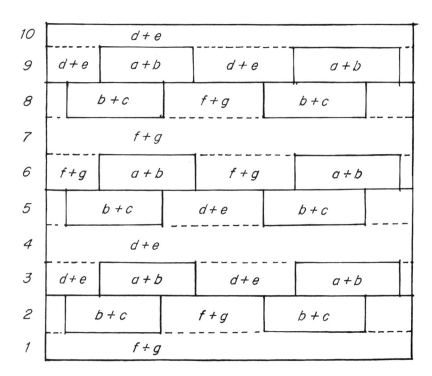

10		d + e		
9	d + e	a + b	d + e	a + b
8	b + c	f + g	b + c	
7		f + g		
6	f + g	a + b	f + g	a + b
5	b + c	d + e	b + c	
4		d + e		
3	d + e	a + b	d + e	a + b
2	b + c	f + g	b + c	
1		f + g		

11.8 Diagram of Sample 1 showing layout and combinations of yarns

1 Key to colour plate – two, three and four shuttle samples

2	3
4	5

lengths were drawn out first on squared paper, and the colouring of the shapes was decided later. This preliminary work is essential to the success of the design. The slits should be positioned so as to ensure a firm and structurally sound fabric. Figure 11.7 illustrates the staggered positions of the slits in Sample 1, and the way in which plain areas are introduced at intervals in the weaving. These areas not only help to create a firmer fabric and a less complex design, but, as mentioned, make the weaving much quicker.

This sample was woven on a 12/15 cotton netting twine, set at 24 ends per 100 mm (6 ends per inch). The weft was natural Welsh 2-ply woollen yarn, doubled throughout. All seven yarns of the range were used in combination, figure 11.8.

After weaving 25 mm (1 in.) in plain weave, (yarns (f) and (g)), the warp was divided into five sections, with two sections for light grey rectangles (b) and (c), and three sections for rectangles in yarns (f) and (g). Two lengths of light grey yarns and three of dark brown were prepared by winding finger hanks, and they were placed in position on the open shed all at the same side of their respective sections of warp, so that weaving could be carried out in *parallel (similar) motion*, figure 11.9(a). This is the term used to describe weaving in which all the yarns pass the same way in the same shed, figure 11.9(b), and the opposite is *contrary motion*, figure 11.10(a) and (b).

Yarns weaving in parallel motion all move in the same direction through the same shed. Each yarn traverses its own block from side to side until the block is the correct height, turning at the

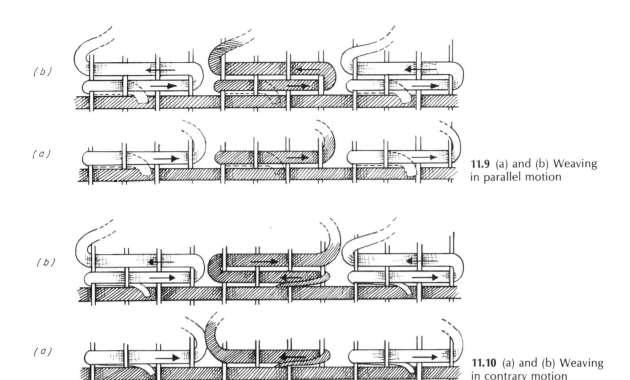

(b)

(a)

11.9 (a) and (b) Weaving in parallel motion

(b)

(a)

11.10 (a) and (b) Weaving in contrary motion

same pair of warp threads at the side of the block in each direction. Beating down can be done either with the fingers or with a weighted fork beater. Alternatively, if the weaving is being done on the loom, the reed can be used for beating, as the work is growing equally over the whole width of the warp. When the required height has been reached, (21 picks in the case of Sample 1), each yarn is passed round the warp thread at the end of its block and turned back through the same shed for two or three threads to fasten it, and then cut off.

Precisely the same process occurs for the next group of rectangles (this time using a mixture of white and grey yarns, figure 11.8, line 3). Again the yarns are placed on the open shed, all at the same side of their respective blocks to weave in parallel motion, the warp threads which are to end the blocks having already been decided upon. This section is followed by a plain dark grey area, the yarn for which can be wound round a shuttle and woven in the normal way.

These three sections comprise the weaving of Sample 1. It will be seen that the light rectangles remain the same throughout, and that the dark shapes and plain stripes create the variation in design and the larger sense of scale.

When a design of this type is being woven it is relatively simple to unpick and re-weave should a mistake be made. It is as well, however, to check carefully the width of the shapes by measuring or by counting the warp threads before too much weaving has been done.

2 Key to colour plate – tie and dye samples

1	2	5
3	4	6

11.11 Sample 2

Sample 2

Sample 2, figure 11.11, was woven in the same yarns as Sample 1. It illustrates how the same design can be woven without long slits by using diagonals, figure 11.12. Firstly 25 mm (1 in.) of plain was woven in the darkest colour, up to the first area of pattern. Then the warp was divided into five areas, three grey (yarns (b) and (c)) and two dark brown (yarns (f) and (g)). The yarns, weaving in parallel motion, went one warp thread further to the right as they went to the right, and one less when going to the left.

This procedure should give the standard angle of 45°. It is important, however, that the beating down should be even and not too severe, otherwise some distortion in the regularity of the shapes will result.

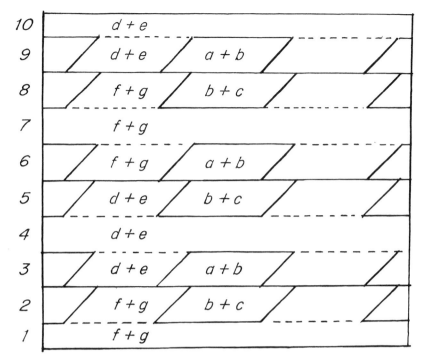

10	d + e			
9	/ d + e / a + b /			/
8	/ f + g / b + c /			/
7	f + g			
6	/ f + g / a + b /			/
5	/ d + e / b + c /			
4	d + e			
3	/ d + e / a + b /			/
2	/ f + g / b + c /			/
1	f + g			

11.12 Diagram of Sample 2 showing layout and combinations of yarns

After completion of the first band of pattern, (24 rows), each yarn was woven back into the same shed and cut off. The next section was then woven in the same way, starting the shapes on the same warp threads as in section 1. As before, the weft threads will shift to the right by one warp thread on each alternate shed, until the right hand point of the diagonal has reached the same warp thread as that at the end of the shape below it. As in Sample 1, section 3 is a plain-weave band, and the pattern continues with small shapes of the same colour, varying only in the arrangement of the background colours.

Sample 3

Before discussing the details of weaving Sample 3, figure 11.13, it is necessary to consider briefly the question of designing on paper for Khelims, which differs considerably from designing tapestries. With a freely painted design which may depend for its effect upon colour mixing and texture, tapestry weaving can achieve a degree of accuracy in translation which is unique.* We are concerned here with the classical Khelim weaver's approach to designing, in particular to the designing of repeating and interlocking shapes to create full scale designs. One of the most effective methods in designing Khelims is to use squared paper, as for designing Ryas.

For Khelims, squared paper with both sets of diagonals drawn in is invaluable, as this provides a grid in which all four directions

*Those readers particularly interested in this aspect of the craft should consult Tadek Beutlich's book *Woven Tapestry* published by Batsford.

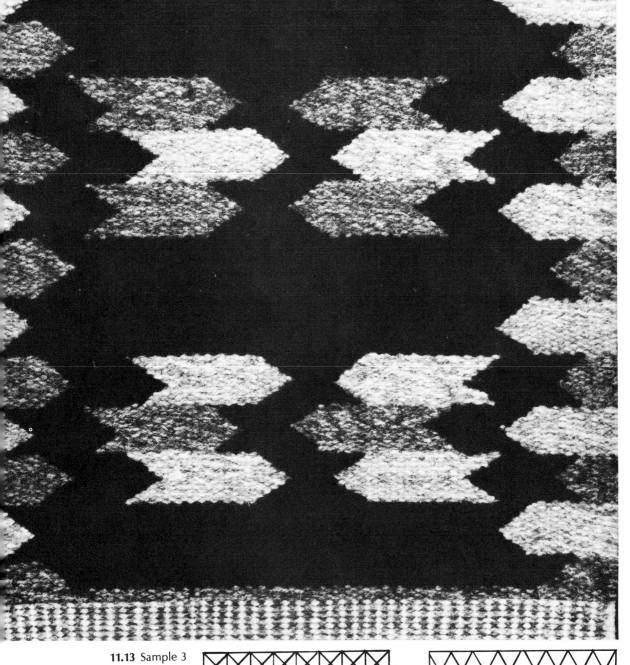

11.13 Sample 3

11.14 (a) and (b) Two
geometric grids

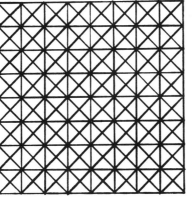

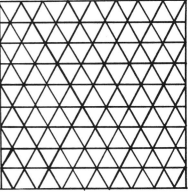

(a)

(b)

11.15 Paper design for Sample 3

are incorporated, figure 11.14(a). Sheets of equilateral triangular grids are equally useful, figure 11.14(b). From these rulings geometric shapes of all kinds can be created.

Designing with cut paper shapes can be equally effective. The designs for Samples 3 and 4 were both achieved in this way, being arrangements of one shape cut out many times. It is better to work out the cut paper shapes on one of the grids referred to, and later draw it up to the required scale. It is possible to combine two or even three shapes in one design but experience will show that one successful shape will provide many variations and secondary shapes, once the process of arranging begins. Shapes should be laid out on the grid from which they were cut, interlocking or overlapping and combining together in larger forms. After each layout, take a tracing of the pattern on transparent grease-proof paper and try another arrangement with the same shapes. Many different arrangements can be made. Later the most promising patterns can be reconstructed from the tracing without much difficulty, and with the satisfaction of knowing that many of the alternatives have been tried. Obtaining a design by this method will result in an outlined pattern, and decisions will have to be made regarding the colour of the shapes before weaving can begin. An excellent method to simplify the problem of deciding on the colours is to begin shading the shapes with a soft pencil, to discover the minimum number of tones that are required to produce the pattern in its new form. It is then not a difficult step to translate the tones into colours, especially if the range of natural yarns already referred to is used.

The design, figure 11.15, for Sample 3 fell naturally into three tones, dark, medium and light. These were translated into the natural Welsh yarns. Four plain yarns were selected rather than the marl yarns and all dyed in a solution of yellow. Three of these were used in two combinations for the two arrow-like shapes, while the background was woven in dark brown.

When weaving a design such as this full-size, the design should itself be drawn out full-size in dark outline. Colours can be indicated with pieces of the actual yarn to be used sellotaped to the shapes, or marked with paint in the shapes. This drawing is called the cartoon, which is hung behind the warp and pinned to the frame, or set up on a board and used to mark the design with a dark felt-tipped pen directly on the warp if a loom is being used. It cannot be fixed behind the warp on a loom, as this would prevent the reed from being used.

Sample 3 used the diagonal of Sample 2, but in both directions. In the arrow-like shapes, the weft yarns progress one warp thread at a time towards the point of the arrow on each pick, discarding one at the other side of the shape at the same time. This continues for 11 rows, when the direction is reversed, shifting one thread in the other direction, discarding the final warp thread on the last pick when it returns to the point from which it started, making 21 picks in all. Figure 11.16 shows the complete process with a reduced number of ends and picks.

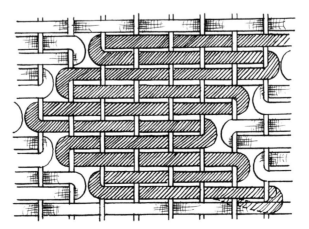

11.16 Weaving arrow-like shapes

Sample 4

Sample 4, figure 11.17, uses a range of fourteen colours in both natural and dyed yarns. Figure 11.18 shows the arrangement of tones. The two ranges are used to give blocks of colour rather than a haphazard scattering of colours. The basic shape is the same as that used in Sample 3, but repeated many more times and covering the whole area of the design. The creation of secondary shapes is caused by the use of mirror repeats down the centre of

11.18 Paper design for sample 4

each group of shapes. The design is composed of two groups of shapes, one light, the other dark, and they are arranged in alternating positions rather like a chess board. The light shapes have been combined to create a much larger form, which, in its way, replaces the areas of plain weaving in the previous samples but not in this one. The light shapes are woven in a slightly darker tone in alternate rows, a device introduced to provide subtlety in what might otherwise become a monotonous rhythm.

The process of designing patterns such as this can be simplified if the main motif is first drawn out several times on separate pieces of paper and positioned in the repeat so that the space between the shapes can be seen. It is a relatively simple problem to fill the spaces that remain with a similar type of shape.

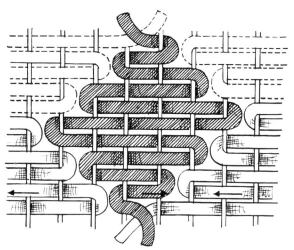

11.19 Weaving diamond shapes (contrary motion)

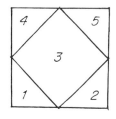

11.20 Order of weaving shapes 1-5

Sample 4 was woven in parallel motion, with the exception of the diamond shapes. The design was drawn up boldly on squared paper to the scale required and placed behind the warp, the edge attached with pins to the first strip of weaving, so that the paper pattern could be raised with the hand behind the warp when required, and released to hang down out of the way when beating up with the reed. This greatly assisted the positioning of each small shape and ensured that all the shapes were of the same size. As the work progressed, the cartoon was wound round the frame of the loom with the weaving.

The weaving of the shapes was carried out precisely as in Sample 3, the only difference being the weaving of the secondary shapes in between the main motifs. Most important of these were the diamonds, the only shapes woven in contrary motion, figure 11.19, which were woven on an even number of warp ends for perfect symmetry.

The weaving of patterns in the manner so far described is advocated especially for those readers weaving Khelim for the first time. It should be mentioned, however, that some weavers prefer weaving and completing one shape at a time before moving on to the next. If this procedure is preferred, the order in which the shapes is woven is an important consideration.

Figure 11.20 shows a simple pattern with the shapes numbered in the order in which they should be woven. This is because no area of the warp should be enclosed by areas of weaving, as it would then be impossible to open a shed and weave it. Unwoven warp must at all times be kept 'open' for the operation of the shed. It is also important, when weaving in this way, to remember that one side of the warp must not be used much more than the other at any stage in the work. Weaving should continue fairly evenly over the whole width of the rug, the maximum amount by which any part should advance more than the rest being about 150 mm (6 in.). To complete the chapter there are descriptions of several techniques which have so far been omitted in the interest of simplicity.

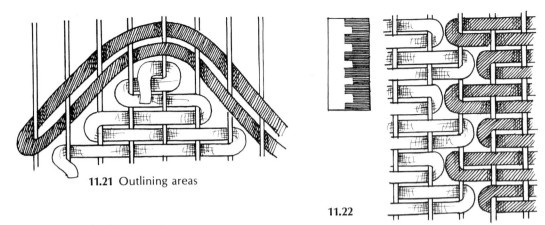

11.21 Outlining areas

11.22 to 11.24 Three vertical colour junctions

11.22

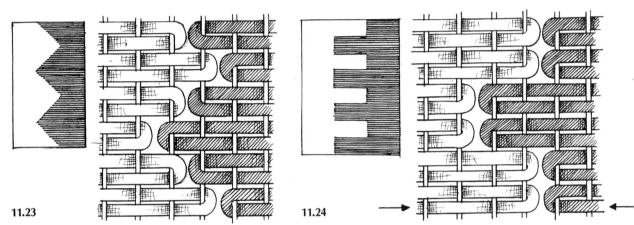

11.23

11.24

Outlining areas

The technique of outlining is illustrated in figure 11.21. It shows how weft yarns can be placed in the warp so that they bend round the shapes, lying in the cloth at an angle to the horizontal line of the normal weft. This technique was used in the past to emphasize a shape, or to imitate a drawn line. It provides opportunities for the designing and weaving of linear patterns as opposed to patterns of shapes. It can create lines that are gentle and curved rather than hard and angular. It is not advisable to use more than six rows together in any one line.

Vertical colour junctions

Figures 11.22, 11.23 and 11.24 illustrate three alternative vertical colour junctions frequently found in classical Khelims. The first of these is the basic method of staggering slits, and the other two are simply variations of this idea. By using this technique, vertical joins can be made of any length instead of being limited to a few rows, as the slit is eliminated. Instead of reversing continually at the same warp thread every time, each weft thread alternates between two adjacent warp threads at successive changes of direction in the first method, progresses in sequence across three warp threads in the second method, and in the third method the weft threads change warp at every second reversal, exaggerating the effect of the first method to make what is called a *brick-join*.

Vertical interlocked wefts

This is one of several Scandinavian methods in which wefts, working in contrary motion, are linked in a chain loop, figure 11.25(a)-(c). This loop occurs in the space between two warp threads, and makes possible the weaving of clearly-defined vertical colour junctions of any length, thus removing the restrictions on design imposed by the practical limits of the length of the open slit, and overcoming the main limitation of the Khelim technique. Khelim provides an excellent foundation on which to build an appreciation of, and a technique for, this type of weaving. Once this has been achieved, innovations of all kinds can be introduced by the craftsman, so that weaving will become much more lively and experimental, and will not be a routine craft governed by a set of rules.

If, in the course of experiment, different types of yarn are used in the same piece of work, it is important to remember that the weight of all the different areas of the cloth must be approximately the same. Failure to observe this will result in distortion and 'bagging', and the rug will not lie flat. Fine yarns can be used if several are woven together as one yarn to increase the weight, and thick yarns can be split up to reduce weight.

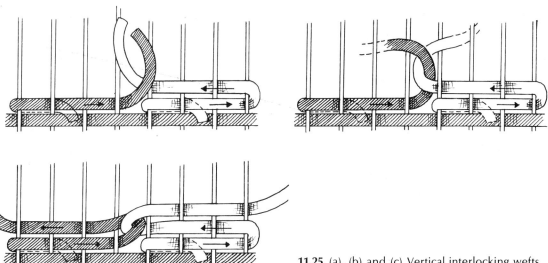

11.25 (a), (b) and (c) Vertical interlocking wefts

12 SOUMAK

Of the three great rug weaving techniques of the East – knotted pile, Khelim and Soumak – it is probably true to say that Soumak is the least well known.

It is interesting to realise that these three as a group clearly represent the constituents of the Basic Design formula, ie spot, shape and line, knotted pile representing the spot, Khelim, shape, and Soumak the element of line.

The name Soumak is said to have derived from the town of Shemaka, at one time the capital of a region in the Caucasus. This area is the chief source of the classical Soumak rugs.

Construction techniques of a similar type have been found in many other parts of the world, the earliest dating from neolithic times.

A type of Soumak weaving known as weft wrapping is still practised by some primitive peoples dwelling in remote parts of S E Asia and by tribes such as the Maori of New Zealand.

In this chapter, Soumak has been combined with two of these closely related methods: Weft chaining and Weft Looping. These techniques are all concerned with the manipulation of weft yarns on the surface of the warp. They are used in a variety of ways to give pattern, texture and weight to the fabric. In all cases plain weaving only is required as a basis to the structure. Wrapping and chaining are carried out with the warp laid flat, making these methods ideal for weaving on simple frames and two shaft looms.

Horizontal Soumak

Figure 12.1(a) illustrates the basic method of weaving Soumak. In this example two wefts are used, one for the surface pattern, the other weaving plain between the rows. This illustration shows the surface yarn being carried over two warp threads, returning back under one. This is called *2/1 locking Soumak*. Figure 12.1(b) shows the same procedure in a non-locking stitch. Differences between locking and non-locking Soumak may at first sight seem slight, but practise will demonstrate that locking Soumak holds the yarn in position as weaving proceeds, while non-locking Soumak does not. In the non-locking type skill is required to ensure that as twining proceeds, each stitch retains its position and the required tension.

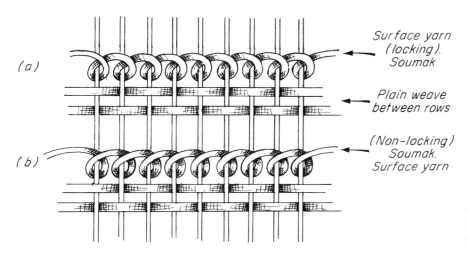

(a)

(b)

Surface yarn
(locking).
Soumak

Plain weave
between rows

(Non-locking)
Soumak.
Surface yarn

12.1 2/1 Soumak (a)
locking (b) non-locking
stitch

Sample 1, figure 12.2, illustrates the appearance of Soumak when woven. The first row (a) shows a 2/1 stitch on three yarns of 2-ply carpet wool. These are loosely twisted before making each stitch to produce a smooth, clear yarn. From this woven example the diagonal line of each stick can be seen. The diagonal ridge can be used effectively to left or right when designing for Soumak. Figure 12.3(a) shows the diagonal ridge running down from left to right. The same yarn returning across the weaving to make another row (b) in locking Soumak will reverse this diagonal. Should the direction of the stitch be required to be the same as the previous row however, it is possible to twine the yarn to produce the same direction (c) but this would result in the non-locking Soumak stitch. In this section of the diagram the two plain picks of weaving between the rows are omitted. Uses of this angling of the Soumak weft can be seen more clearly on the following two colour effects of Sample 1.

Sample 1 shows a variation of the 2/1 sequence in the second woven line (b). This is a 4/2 locking Soumak illustrated in diagrammatic form in figure 12.4. Rows (c) and (d) of Sample 1 are attempts to increase the width of the woven ridge. Here a Soumak twining round two warp ends is used, hence the term Double Soumak. Figures 12.5 and 12.6 illustrate the method of weaving.

A characteristic of Soumak weaving is the method of floating the yarn at the back of the fabric where one line of weaving ends and another begins. On completion of a line the yarn is not cut off but carried behind the weaving to its new position. This process means that, like knotted pile, Soumak weaving has a face and reverse side. It is important that these floats are not too long, 50 mm (2 in.) being about the limit if the weaving is to be practical. This characteristic in turn imposes certain limitations on the weaving which must be taken into account when designing patterns for Soumak. In Sample 1(e) the method of weaving solid shapes is illustrated. This has been woven in a 2/1 Soumak with two picks of plain weaving between the rows. Figure 12.7 shows the way in

12.2 Sample 1

k

j

i

h

g

f

e

d

c

b

a

110

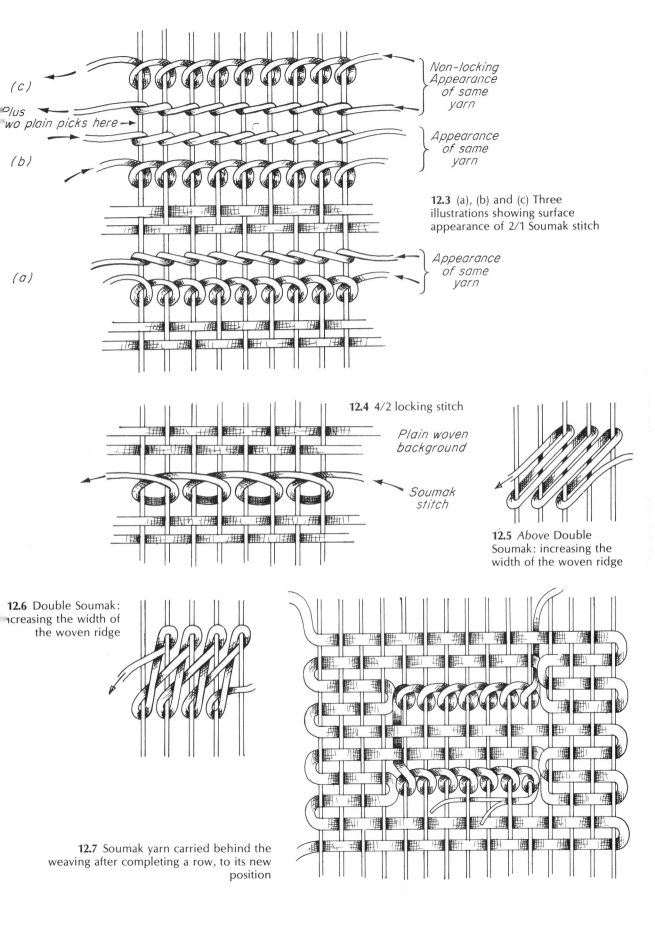

(c)

Non-locking Appearance of same yarn

Plus two plain picks here →

(b)

Appearance of same yarn

12.3 (a), (b) and (c) Three illustrations showing surface appearance of 2/1 Soumak stitch

Appearance of same yarn

(a)

Appearance of same yarn

12.4 4/2 locking stitch

Plain woven background

Soumak stitch

12.5 *Above* Double Soumak: increasing the width of the woven ridge

12.6 Double Soumak: increasing the width of the woven ridge

12.7 Soumak yarn carried behind the weaving after completing a row, to its new position

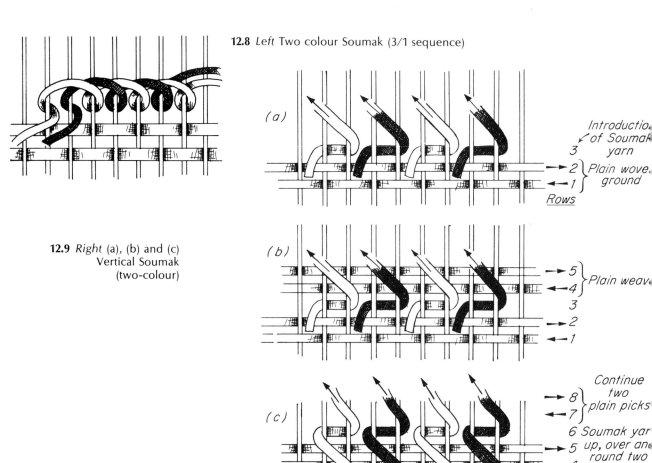

12.8 *Left* Two colour Soumak (3/1 sequence)

(a)

Introductio[n]
of Soumak
yarn

3

→ 2 } Plain wove[n]
← 1 } ground

Rows

12.9 *Right* (a), (b) and (c)
Vertical Soumak
(two-colour)

(b)

→ 5 } Plain weav[e]
← 4

3

→ 2
← 1

(c)

Continue
two
plain picks

→ 8
→ 7

6 Soumak yar[n]
→ 5 up, over an[d]
round two
← 4 warp threa[ds]
3
→ 2
← 1

Black Soumak
yarn continuing
up and over
2 more warp
threads, behind
2 warp threads

12.10 Vertical Soumak.
Changing colour positions

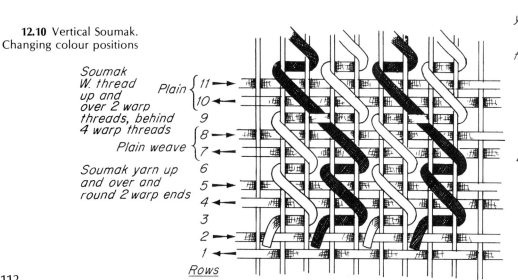

Soumak
W. thread
up and
over 2 warp
threads, behind
4 warp threads

Plain { 11 →
       { 10 ←
         9

Plain weave { 8 →
            { 7 ←

Soumak yarn up
and over and
round 2 warp ends

6
5 →
4 ←
3
2 →
1 ←

Rows

Soumak
Black thread
up and over
2 warp threads,
behind *White*
Soumak yarn

which both shuttles are used, with the yarn weaving the Soumak stitch floating behind the weaving to its new position at the end of each row, and the background yarn weaving an additional pick either side to bring the weaving up to the same level.

Section (e), Sample 1, uses, for the sake of convenience, a simple rectangle, but it must be appreciated that Soumak is capable of weaving all types of geometrical shapes in much the same way as Khelim. Instead of keeping to a vertical line each side, the rows of Soumak could have followed a diagonal course, or stepped or zig-zagged in a variety of ways. Drawing lines to represent rows of Soumak on squared graph paper can provide many arrangements of horizontal stripes for this purpose.

The woven Sample 2 (colour plate 3 facing page 120) uses the idea of stripes and rectangular shapes taken from these first five sections of Sample 1. This has been woven throughout in a 2/1 Soumak, beginning with six plain picks of a brown 2-ply woollen yarn doubled, and six picks of background coloured yarns before weaving the first rows of Soumak. There are eight picks of back-ground plain weave between the single rows of Soumak. By the reversing of alternate sections of stripes and rectangles the scale of the pattern is increased as the shapes come together in larger areas.

Returning to Sample 1, line (f) illustrates a two-colour single Soumak in a 2/1 sequence. Figure 12.8 shows the method of weav-ing, the locking type of Soumak being used. Sections (g) and (h) show two ways in which blocks of two-colour Soumak can be arranged by using the two directions of the diagonal ridge. In all other respects the method of weaving is the same as for single colour Soumak, including methods of introducing the yarn, and floating behind the weaving to the new position.

Vertical Soumak

In section (i) Sample 1, the two-colour principle is used in a vertical Soumak. Figure 12.9(a), (b) and (c) illustrates how this works, twining one row at a time. Yarns drawn in black and white indicate the two colours. Figure 12.10 demonstrates the method of changing colour positions and figures 12.11 and 12.12 the methods of working diagonally. These techniques can be quite complicated to weave without prior experience and it is essential to begin by practising them on small samples before attempting a full scale design. When these stitches have been mastered they will be found quicker and more fascinating to weave than pre-vious methods. The stitch is bolder and the scale more appropriate to a floor covering.

Description of Sample 3

In this sample (colour plate 3 facing age 120) vertical Soumak and its two associated diagonals are used from sections (i), (j) and (k) of Sample 1. In this sample however, the vertical Soumak stitches

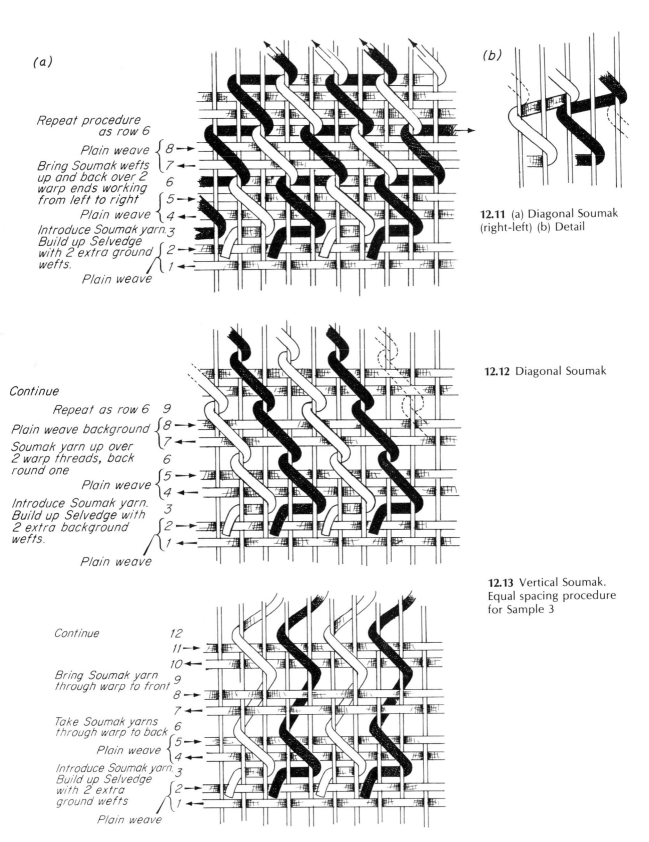

(a)

Repeat procedure
as row 6

Plain weave { 8 →
Bring Soumak wefts 7 ←
up and back over 2
warp ends working 6
from left to right
{ 5 →
Plain weave { 4 ←
Introduce Soumak yarn. 3
Build up Selvedge { 2 →
with 2 extra ground
wefts. { 1 ←
Plain weave

(b)

12.11 (a) Diagonal Soumak
(right-left) (b) Detail

Continue

Repeat as row 6   9
Plain weave background { 8 →
{ 7 ←
Soumak yarn up over 6
2 warp threads, back
round one
Plain weave { 5 →
{ 4 ←
Introduce Soumak yarn. 3
Build up Selvedge with
2 extra background { 2 →
wefts. { 1 ←
Plain weave

12.12 Diagonal Soumak

12.13 Vertical Soumak.
Equal spacing procedure
for Sample 3

Continue   12
11 →
10 ←
Bring Soumak yarn 9
through warp to front 8 →
7 ←
Take Soumak yarns 6
through warp to back { 5 →
Plain weave { 4 ←
Introduce Soumak yarn. 3
Build up Selvedge { 2 →
with 2 extra
ground wefts { 1 ←
Plain weave

114

have been woven with an additional pair of plain picks. This can be seen at row six, figure 12.13. This technique succeeds in opening out the line of vertical stitches to introduce more of the coloured background and gives a greater sense of continuity between vertical and diagonal stitches. Figure 12.13 shows the method of weaving. Sample 3 also gives some idea of one of the many ways in which these three directions of vertical Soumak may be used.

Beginning to weave

In all the Soumak woven samples brown/grey camel hair warp was used at 16 double ends per 100 mm (4 double ends per inch). To provide a dark edging to the weaving a plain brown woollen yarn similar in colour to the warp was used in the weft for the first 12 picks, in two 2-ply yarns. The coloured background yarn was then introduced and this is a combination of four threads; two of 2-ply carpet wool, one singles woollen yarn and a fancy looped mohair yarn, in all a combination of yarns in four different colours, the looped mohair providing a distinctive yet subtle surface texture. The same four colours are used in the surface Soumak pattern but separated into their similar tones. The four background yarns were wound together onto one shuttle and introduced for six picks before the first line of Soumak. This was introduced into the central area of the sample, the background plain weave being built up either side, figure 12.7, to bring the weaving to the same level before continuing. As almost all illustrations show, at least two plain picks are used between each row of Soumak when weaving solid areas, to ensure a sound foundation to the weaving. More of the plain woven ground can be used, of course, where more space is required.

Beginning and ending Soumak stitch is also illustrated in figure 12.7. It is done by splitting the yarn and separating the ply, and then tapering the end by cutting by degrees.

Weft chaining

Weft chaining has the appearance of two rows of closely woven Soumak stitch, but has the advantage of being much more rapid to weave.

As with Soumak, two separate sets of yarn are required, one for the background weave and the other for the decorative chaining. Figure 12.14 illustrates the method of weaving chain stitch in a series of four drawings (a), (b), (c) and (d). In the first, (a), the chaining yarn is carried along with the woven background to the point where the first stitch is to be made. Here the shed is closed and the yarn passed *through* the warp to continue in the same direction *behind* the warp threads. Chaining is carried out by the thumb and first finger of the right hand, picking the yarn through (in this case) alternate warp threads (b and c), until the required

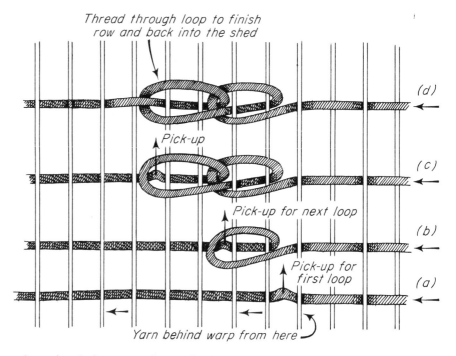

Thread through loop to finish
row and back into the shed

(d)

Pick-up

(c)

Pick-up for next loop

(b)

Pick-up for
first loop

(a)

Yarn behind warp from here

12.14 (a), (b), (c) and (d)
Weft chaining. One-
colour on alternate spaces

length of chain is achieved. The final stitch (d) is made by thread-ing the yarn *through the final loop*. The shed can then be opened for the yarn to continue its way along with the background yarn to the selvedge.

The skill required in weaving chain stitch is in the weaver's ability to create an evenly tensioned stitch along the length of the chain. Each loop must not be too tight or the weaving will become distorted, nor must the loop be too slack, in which case weaving appears untidy and unprofessional. It is all a matter of skilfully manipulating the yarn with the fingers to obtain just the right length of loop each time in the chains. Chains can be woven with a fine or coarser stitch, depending on the weight of yarn used. A finer yarn will require a finer stitch chaining round each warp thread, while a coarser yarn can be chained round the second or third warp thread. Woven sample 4, section (a) illustrates the woven appearance of a one-colour chain stitch.

Sample 4, figure 12.15, section (c) shows a two-colour chain stitch. Here the procedure is the same as for one colour, but with the addition of another yarn – in this case a dark red. Figure 12.16 illustrates this method of weaving.

Weaving solid shapes

As with Soumak, weaving close rows of chain stitch can create solid shapes. Again for convenience, Sample 4(b) shows a simple rectangle, but as with Soumak, chain stitch can be used to weave many different geometrical shapes. This is demonstrated in Sample 5 (colour plate 3 facing page 120), where chain stitch is used to produce a design in which two staggered lines are arran-

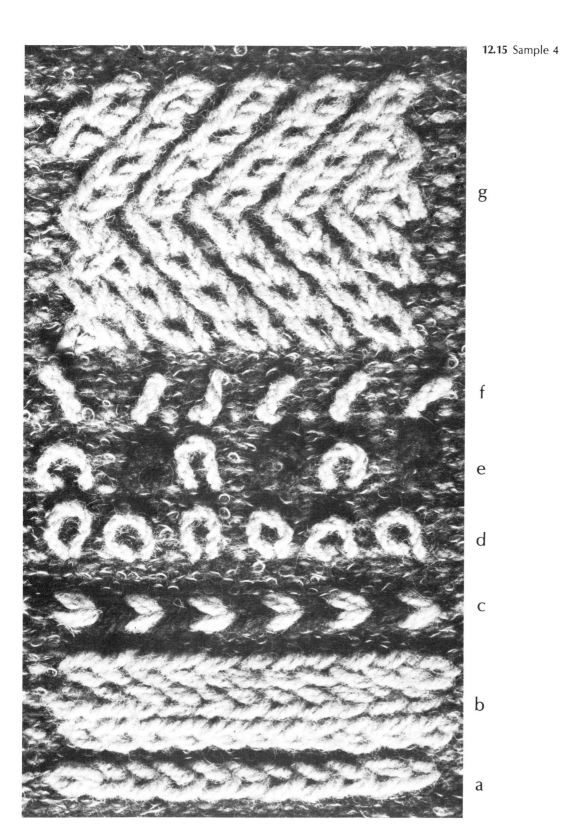

g

f

e

d

c

b

a

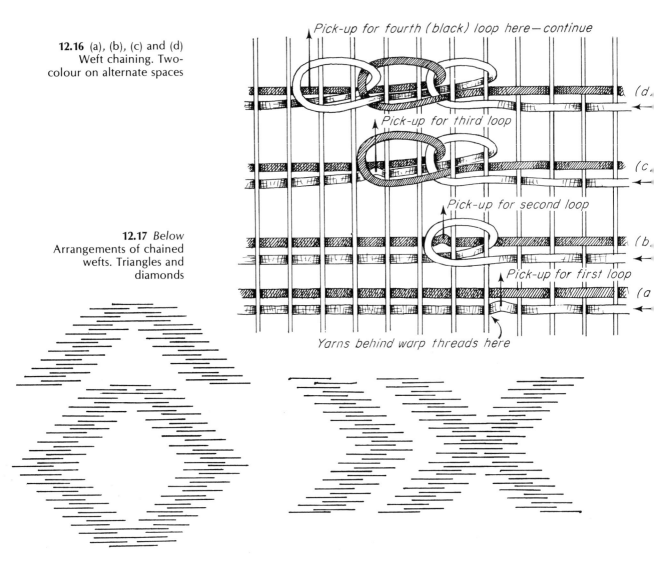

12.16 (a), (b), (c) and (d) Weft chaining. Two-colour on alternate spaces

Pick-up for fourth (black) loop here—continue

Pick-up for third loop

12.17 *Below* Arrangements of chained wefts. Triangles and diamonds

Pick-up for second loop

Pick-up for first loop

(d,

(c,

(b,

(a

Yarns behind warp threads here

12.18 *Right* Arrangements of chained wefts. Crosses and zigzags

ged diagonally across the weaving. This idea could of course be worked out in a number of different ways. Figures 12.17 and 12.18 demonstrate two of these, using diamond shapes, triangles, crosses and zigzags.

Weft looping

Weft looping is a simple but effective method of decorating a plain-woven cloth. The method illustrated by the woven example (d), Sample 4 is basically the same as weaving for Soumak or chain stitch. As before, two shuttles are used, one for the plain woven ground and the other for the loops. Begin by weaving approximately twelve rows of plain background before introducing loops. After the shuttle of loop yarns has been thrown *keep the shed open* and pull up loops on alternate *raised* warp ends,

118

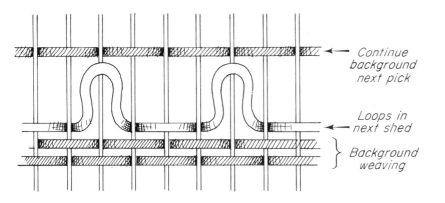

Continue background next pick

Loops in next shed

} Background weaving

Continue: plain background weave

} 2 separate yarn for loops in same shed

Plain woven background. At least 12 rows before first row of loops

12.19 Weft looping. One-colour. Loops pulled up on alternate spaces

12.20 *Below left* Weft looping. Two-colour

12.21 *Below* (a) and (b) Weft looping. Two basic positions

(a)

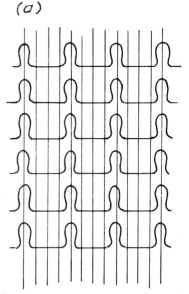

(b)

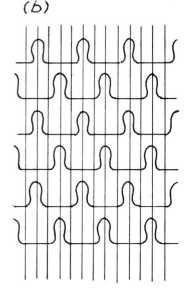

figure 12.19. To ensure that loops are equal in length, they can be threaded over the end of a shed stick as looping proceeds. The stick should not be removed until after the next plain woven (background) pick, so that the loops are held in position by the plain weaving.

In section (e) of the woven Sample 4, the introduction of a second coloured loop is illustrated, figure 12.20. This is a simple method of adding variety to the pattern of loops using two loop threads of contrasting colours in the same shed. They can be wound onto one shuttle or kept separate depending on how regularly they are to be used.

There are two basic positions for arranging loops. These are illustrated in figure 12.21(a) and (b). In terms of design these would be straight and half-drop repeats. The secret of designing with either of these two positions is to arrange them around a basic shape or series of shapes, taking into account the background area or space. Gaps left in the pattern of loops give the sense of interrupted rhythm, and by leaving a larger space, a contrast is provided between loops and plain woven ground.

Creating symmetrical shapes requires an odd number of warp ends. This provides a central thread and means that triangular shapes can be constructed which begin and end in a single loop. Most simple patterns can be worked out on the warp by counting warp threads and indicating the position of shapes by tying knots

2	3
5	6

3 Key to colour plate –
Soumak samples

around warp threads with short pieces of yarn. Shapes can also be drawn onto the warp with a soft pencil or felt-tipped pen before weaving begins. Sample 6, colour plate 3, shows weft looping.

Hand plied yarns

Although looping can be done with any existing 2- or 6-ply yarns, the examples illustrated in Sample 4 have been woven with a combination of two 2-ply yarns plied or twisted together by hand to produce a thread which is thicker than a normal 2-ply rug yarn and firmer to handle than a 6-ply carpet yarn.

As plying threads by twisting causes a shortening in the length of the yarn, it is as well to produce a fair amount each time. In the case of the yarn for Sample 4, 3.5 mm (12 ft) of two 2-ply threads were twisted to produce approximately 1.8 m (6 ft) of 4-ply yarn.

Twisting can be carried out very simply by using a carpenter's hand drill fitted with a large crochet hook, or with the hook tied to the spindle of a bobbin winder, if such is available.

The process of twisting commences by knotting both ends of the two 2-ply yarns, one end being passed over the hook of the drill/winder, the other being held firmly in position by means of a wall hook or some other permanent fixture. The centre of the yarns being plied must be clearly marked. A short piece of thread knotted firmly in position is ideal.

A considerable amount of twist must be put into the yarn, making sure at the same time that it is spread evenly throughout the whole length. Having achieved this, the two ends of the twisted threads are brought together, without releasing the tension, the yarn being folded at the central point, which is held until the two halves of the yarn are brought together. When it is released the twist will cause the two yarns to twine together instantly, the firmness of the twining being dependent upon the amount of twist in the yarn.

In section (f) of the woven Sample 4 a line of loops illustrates another twining method where the twining takes place on the individual loop. This is achieved by twisting a thread as described and winding it straight onto the shuttle, keeping the yarn under tension the whole time. When weaving begins it may be necessary

12.22 Weft looping.
Twisted loops

Spacing between rows of loops increased by greater number of plain picks. Odd number if loops to stay on same set of warp threads

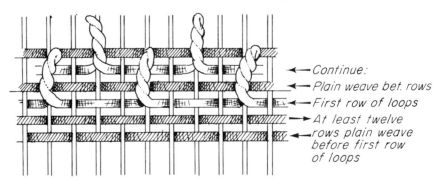

←—*Continue:*
←—*Plain weave bet. rows*
←—*First row of loops*
→—*At least twelve*
←—*rows plain weave before first row of loops*

to add twist again to the end of the yarn with the fingers. Precautions must be taken so that the yarn remains twined. After the required number of plain woven wefts have been inserted, the twisted yarn can be introduced into the warp. Twining will take place as the loops are pulled up in the weaving. Figure 12.22 illustrates this method of weaving diagrammatically.

Chained loops

In the final section (g) of Sample 4, the process of chaining and looping is combined in a technique called chained loops, figure 12.23.

This technique involves two stages: first the weaving of the lines of loops, and second the process of chaining the loops together by hand.

In the first process the loops must be woven to produce the correct length of loop for chaining to take place. This means that the loops must be long enough to overlap one another comfortably. If they are too short the weaving will be distorted, if too long the clear, neat links of the chain will not be clearly seen. In the woven sample loops were threaded onto a 20 mm (⁷⁄₈ in.) shed stick. Five picks of background weaving with two 2-ply yarns were woven between the rows of loops.

Designing with loops can be done to make chains follow certain set patterns. The staggered half-drop position gives a diagonal chain, while for a vertical chain the straight repeat position is required.

Note Weaving with a number of surface yarns and incorporating them into the background weaving may result in problems occurring where yarns are taken round selvedge threads. If this is so, reference should be made to chapter 9 *Two, three and four shuttle techniques*, which provides in detail solutions to these problems.

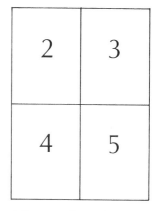

4 Key to colour plate – warp-faced weave samples

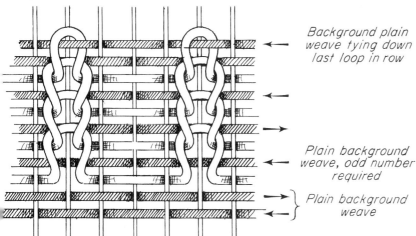

Background plain weave tying down last loop in row

Plain background weave, odd number required

Plain background weave

12.23 Chained loops

121

13 WARP-FACED WEAVES

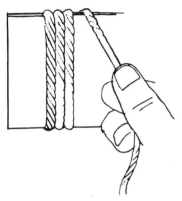

13.1 Winding yarn round cardboard strips

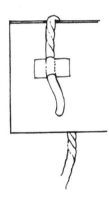

13.2 Back view. Transparent adhesive tape holding ends in position

All the weaving methods so far considered have been weft-faced weaves, the weft yarn creating the surface of the fabric and completely covering the warp. In warp-faced weaves, the warp creates the surface of the fabric by completely covering the weft. To achieve this, the warp yarns have to be thicker and more closely set. In the samples, woollen yarns of 6-ply, or cable of 3/2-ply were used, set at 50 ends per 100 mm (12 ends per inch).

Designing the warp

Designing for a warp-faced weave means in effect designing the warp. Warp designs are normally arrangements of stripes of differently-coloured yarns, the only exceptions being when multi-coloured yarns are being used and the colours are not continuous, Sample 5 (colour plate 4 facing page 121).

Stripes can be designed either on paper by painting the colours or cutting out strips of coloured paper and pasting them down, or by using the actual yarns that are already dyed to the required colours, and winding them round a strip of card. This is an excellent way of representing the surface of a warp, and warps can be planned quickly and with the minimum of yarn, figure 13.1. The ends of the yarns at colour-changes are held with small pieces of self-adhesive tape on the back of the card, figure 13.2. Yarns can be wound singly to the required width, or in groups of three or four colours to repeat the same sequence each time, figure 13.3(a). Designing warps, however, is not as simple as it may first appear, and many alterations may be needed in a pattern before a satisfactory result is achieved. The samples for this chapter underwent many changes before they were finally woven.

The samples illustrate two methods of arranging the colours in a warp.

(a) Random colour sequence – in which yarns are arranged at random, the designer relying on intuition alone.

(b) Numerical colour sequence – in which yarns follow a set pattern, and change order or progress only as the method allows.

Samples 1, figure 13.5, 2 and 3 (colour plate 4 facing page 121) are from one warp based on a random colour sequence, while Samples 4 and 5 (colour plate 4 facing page 121) are on a warp-based numerical progression, in which the order of the colours is frequently reversed, figures 13.3(b) and (c). In both cases the success or failure of the design depends mainly on the overall general proportions, that is areas of light and dark, areas of pattern or texture, and the colour combinations. A problem arises in this method of designing when a single warp thread is to be used, instead of a pair. It takes two warp threads to create the effect of a line in the cloth and one yarn by itself weaves a succession of small spots, an effect that it is impossible to create on the card. The only way to overcome this is to use a thinner yarn to represent the single yarn. While this does not provide an accurate representation of the woven spot, it acts as a reminder to the weaver when preparing the warp, that a single end is to be used.

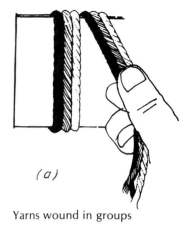

(a)

Yarns wound in groups

Colour

All the woven samples were planned around colour schemes based on blue. This gives a choice of blues ranging from purple and mauve on the red side of the scale, to cerulean and turquoise on the yellow side of the scale. From this range four colours were selected, sufficiently different from each other to be clearly seen, and in each colour four separate hanks were dyed in four distinct tones, from pale to very dark, thus giving sixteen different blues to choose from, many of them being directly related to one another.

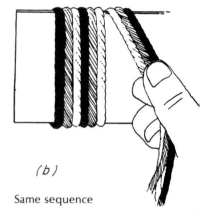

(b)

Same sequence

Weaving

Weaving a full-sized rug in this technique is best carried out on a loom. With so many thick warp yarns, difficulties will be encountered in attempting to work on a frame, especially with tensioning and shedding.

Preparing the warp

As the warp for this weave is made up of such heavy yarns, warping is best done directly on the loom. Generally, warps for warp weaves are for one or two rugs only, so that the length of the warp is shorter than for other weaves. Yarns can be tied to the back stick individually, or in groups of four or six, and each one passed through the shed sticks, heddles and reed in one operation.

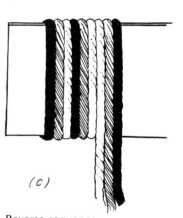

(c)

Reverse sequence

13.3 (a), (b) and (c)

Warp tension

Special care must be taken to ensure that the tension on all the warp threads is perfectly even before weaving starts. Correcting the tension for this type of warp is impossible once weaving has begun. Always weave a few rows of waste after tying up, to make sure that there are no inconsistencies in the tension. These will show where the weft yarn fails to remain straight however much pressure is placed upon it by the batten. Readers who have not had previous experience of this method of weaving are advised to make a small-scale sample first. Warps 250 mm - 300 mm (10 in. - 12 in.) wide are well suited to this exercise. Even with a warp as narrow as 300 mm (12 in.), a total of 150 (144) 6-ply ends are required.

Weft yarns

The number and ply of weft yarns is varied according to the effect required and to the thickness needed in the finished rug. In general however, wefts range from a single two-ply yarn to a combination of three or four 6-ply yarns. Information relating to the different uses of weft thicknesses can be found under the notes for the woven samples.

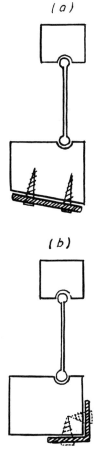

(a)

(b)

13.4 (a) and (b) Additional weight for batten (race block)

Shedding

Shedding a warp of this density can present problems, and special care must be taken to ensure that all the warp yarns are in their correct position when weaving. Woollen yarns often matt together, and separating heavy woollen warp threads for each new shed can be a slow process. However, as fewer picks are required per centimeter (inch) weaving will grow at a similar pace to more conventional weaves.

Reeding

Reeding a warp of this weight cannot be done on a reed of the same sett as the warp at one end per dent. The threads are too thick to allow the reed to move easily, and the friction will generate fluff, which will in turn cause more trouble by making it difficult to separate the threads. Instead, the warp ends are threaded two or three to a dent in a reed of half or one-third of the sett, so that the yarns can move freely past each other. Care must be taken when threading that yarns are not crossed between the heddles and the reed, and that no irregularities or weaknesses occur in any of the warp threads.

Beating

Because of the thickness of the warp, extra effort must be made to ensure that the weft yarns are beaten up as closely as possible. To achieve this it may be necessary to add extra weight to the batten in the form of a metal strip drilled with holes at intervals and screwed to the underside of the race block, figure 13.4(a) and (b), or to use a metal hand beater to give additional pressure to the weft.

The woven samples

Sample 1, figure 13.5, illustrates the three basic effects obtained from plain warp-faced weave. They will be recognised instantly as identical to their weft-faced counterparts, (i) warp stripes, (ii) weft stripes, and (iii) spots.

Variations of colour, proportion and width can be used in an unlimited number of ways in warp stripes. Areas (a), (b) and (c) illustrate some of these. Weft stripes are obtained by placing alternate light and dark single yarns in the warp, area (d). Alternative positions are obtained by placing two similarly toned yarns together. Spots are introduced in the weft in two ways, (e) being one light yarn in every four to produce light spots on a dark background in equally-spaced lines, and (f) being one dark yarn in three to give an all-over spot effect on a light background. The weft consists of three 6-ply yarns wound onto one shuttle, and woven in plain weave. When weaving, weft yarns can be pulled tightly through the shed, being careful to avoid distorting the selvedge. Weft yarns do not have to lie in an arc before being beaten down, as in other weaves, as it is the warp that has to bend round the weft in a warp-faced fabric, and not the other way round as in the more usual weft-faced ones.

Sample 2 (colour plate 4 facing page 121) woven on the same warp, illustrates the effect when two contrasting weft yarns are used, one thick (three 6-ply), and one thin (two 2-ply). It also illustrates how the surface texture is changed by emphasizing certain yarns and reducing the importance of others. This gives the effect of colour blocks involving spots of different sizes. The emphasis is reversed by using two thick and two thin yarns consecutively in two successive sheds.

In Sample 3 (colour plate 4 facing page 121) the same warp is transformed by re-tying the treadles of the loom to weave a $\frac{3}{1}$ twill. Figure 13.6 shows how each warp thread floats over three picks and under one. The thickness of the weft yarn remains constant with three 6-ply yarns in each row, wound onto one shuttle.

Note In weaving this twill, plain weave was introduced between each twill shed using a single 2-ply thread. This helped to create a much firmer weave.

Samples 4 and 5 (colour plate 4 facing page 121) were both woven on a warp designed by numerical colour sequence. Four coloured yarns were wound round a strip of card in strict order, reversing positions at the third wind. This method produced groups of single and double colour lines in unexpected positions. These samples use a weaving technique in which the weft floats over the warp threads in places, to produce weft spots. These spots can be in a contrasting yarn or colour, or as in Sample 4, can be used simply to stop out parts of the pattern stripes. This effect is

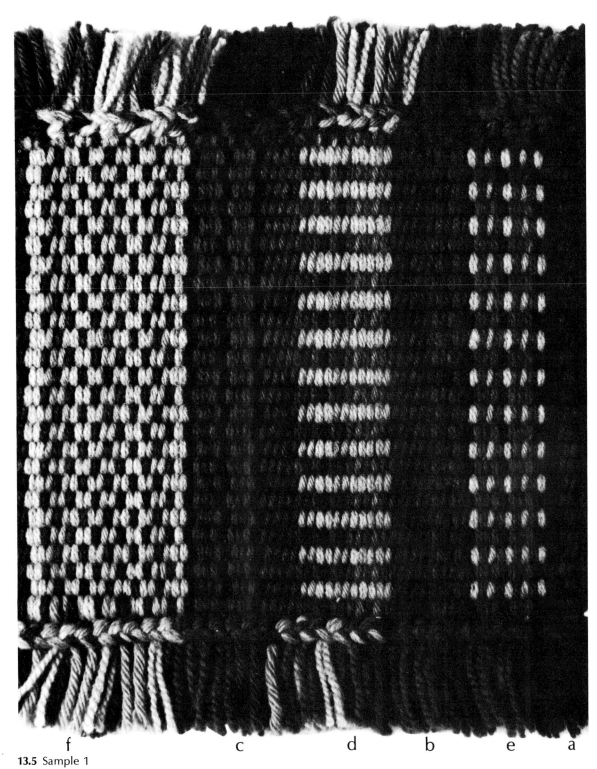

f   c   d   b e a

13.5 Sample 1

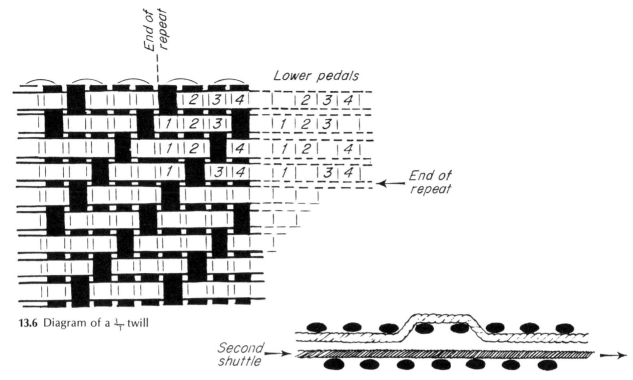

13.6 Diagram of a $\frac{3}{1}$ twill

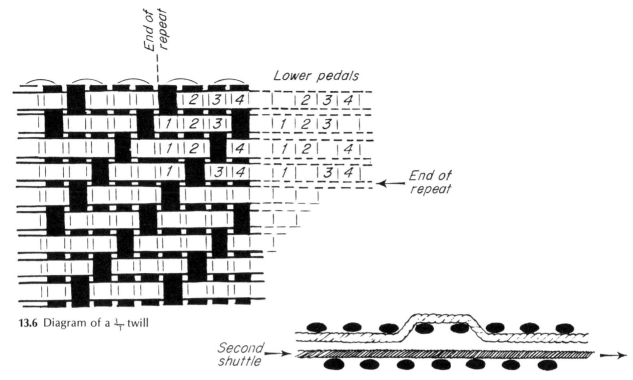

13.7 Weft floats over warp faced weave

achieved by selecting one of the colours of the warp, and winding yarns of this colour onto a shuttle in sufficient thickness to cover the warp threads; in this case three 2-ply yarns were wound together. Figure 13.7 shows the method of floating the weft yarns over the warp when required, the shuttle being brought out of the shed at the beginning of the spot, passed across the surface of the warp for the length of the spot, and replaced in the shed at the end of the spot. This is done with the shed open, the groups of threads for the weave being selected by hand, and the shuttle being passed in and out of the shed across the warp, rather like the process of sewing with a needle and thread. To compensate for the gaps in the shed, a second shuttle is prepared with a finer yarn to weave through each successive shed, to provide a firm, sound weave. Sample 4 illustrates how a straightforward stripe can be transformed into a pattern of lines which stop and start, narrow and widen again in a variety of ways.

In Sample 5 this process is taken to its limits. The weft yarns are changed according to the warp colour sequence and held in position by warp yarns of the same colour. The idea is to create an illusion so that the warp stripes appear to change direction and travel over or under one another.

Care must be taken, if such a method is used, to ensure that the weft floats are not too long. It must be admitted that certain sections of Sample 5, where long floats are held in position by the minimum of weft yarns, make the design impractical for floor covering. To be practical, weft floats should not exceed 25 mm (1 in.) in length. Were this sample to be woven as a rug, changes would have to be made in the design to rectify this weakness.

127

14 MATTING

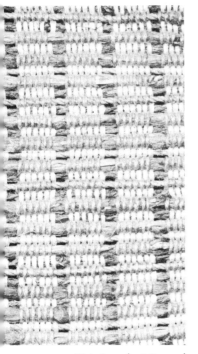

14.1 Sample 1 Spaced warp (woven by Peter Collingwood)

Under the heading *Matting*, this chapter introduces the range of natural (vegetable) fibres and man-made materials available to the rug weaver. These can be used in place of the more conventional woollen yarns and provide opportunities for an altogether more experimental type of fabric.

Vegetable fibres include hemp, jute, flax (linen), cotton, sisal, coconut fibre (coir), seagrass, rushes, and raffia. These materials can be purchased in a wide range of types and weights. Materials such as jute, hemp and flax, for example, can be obtained in their rough unspun state. Fine quality cotton and linen yarns are available from suppliers in a wide range of colours. These can be plyed or plaited to produce different weights and unusual colour combinations to meet specific needs.

Yarn of sisal, hemp and jute can be purchased in a number of different weights from types of string to lightweight rope. The latter provides some of the most promising heavy yarns for this type of weaving. Many of these materials can also be dyed. Yarns instantly recognisable in their natural colours become transformed and difficult to identify when, for example, dyed in a contrasting tone.

Under the heading man-made materials come plastics, rayon, nylon, metallic yarns, cellophane and paper.

This chapter uses the weaving techniques explained in previous sections, encouraging the production of different designs by the use of these materials, in place of wool. Plain weave is used extensively.

Many of the woven samples in plain weave illustrate the way in which matting designs can be created from the materials themselves. The design skill required here is to be found in the proportion of each part.

A recurring feature of this type of weave is the tendency for the warp to be seen floating on the surface of the weaving. This is invariably due to the inflexible nature of the weft in that the yarns cannot be beaten down sufficiently to cover the warp. To produce a more stable weave, fine cotton or linen yarns are frequently used between the picks. These finer yarns provide opportunities to introduce small quantities of contrasting texture or spots of bright colour to enliven the general effect.

Two ways in which the exposed warp has been made a feature of

the design can be seen in Samples 1 and 2.

Sample 1, figure 14.1, uses a hemp yarn in what is known as a *spaced* warp. In this, small areas of the reed are left blank and the warp threads appear to be grouped in blocks. As the weft yarn spans the gaps in the warp, it is left exposed and at these points the quality of the yarn can be clearly seen. As with split tapestry, care must be taken in using this technique that gaps in the warp do not exceed 25 mm (1 in.). Gaps wider than this tend to become impractical for rugs. In this design the space represents four warp ends.

In Sample 2, figure 14.2, variety is obtained by the use of white and coloured warp yarns. These yarns are grouped in blocks of two contrasting tones. This is set at 16 double ends per 100 mm (4 double ends per inch) and uses plaited rushes, cotton and dyed coir.

Rushes, being a hard material (unless fresh), are soaked in luke-warm water before use. Joins in the rushes should be engineered along the centre of the shed, the rushes turned at the selvedge to create a continuous strip. Care should be taken to ensure that these loops are not too long, 50 mm (2 in.) being about the maximum space between rows. Should a wider gap be required, rushes should be cut at the end of the row and begun again. Experience will show, however, that a design in which the material is con-

14.2 Sample 2 Dyed warp 1-1 plaited rush

129

tinuously looped along the selvedge is more practical and has a more professional appearance than if cut at the end of each row.

In this section are also included designs which use rag as the main weaving material. This was at one time one of the most popular and inexpensive ways of making rugs. Any piece of cloth can be used, although dark strong colours are more practical than light pale ones. Strips of rag can be woven in plain weave or twill to produce a flat hardwearing fabric. Interesting multicoloured effects can be produced by threading any number of small pieces, contrasting in colour, into the shed as a continuous strip. If this is done care must be taken to ensure that the amount of material in the shed at one time is equal across the width of the weaving. A firmer fabric is obtained by weaving a fine cotton or linen yarn between the rows (Sample 3, figure 14.5). Cutting large pieces of cloth into a continuous strip can be achieved by following the diagram, figure 14.3.

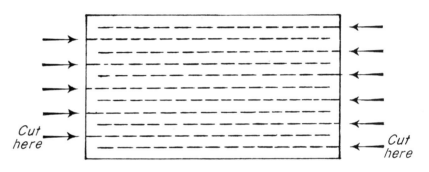

Cut here

Cut here

14.3 *Right* Cutting rag into continuous strip

The flat-woven rag rug, Sample 3, figure 14.5, was woven in two strips of coloured rag one 12 mm (½ in.) the other 6 mm (¼ in.) wide on a warp of camel hair 16 double ends per mm (4 double ends per inch) in plain weave.

In this sample the 12 mm (½ in.) strip is a combination of three different coloured rags prepared beforehand by cutting into short lengths and gluing together in a pre-arranged order. This created a multi-coloured continuous rag yarn.

The pieces of rag to be cut must first be ironed flat, and the widths and lengths drawn on the cloth as a rectangular grid with a soft pencil. These can then all be cut out with a pair of sharp scissors. The 12 mm (½ in.) strips in this sample were cut in two sizes, 50 mm and 100 mm (2 in. and 4 in.) long and glued together in a set order with Copydex adhesive overlapping 6 mm (¼ in.).

An efficient system for assembling small pieces of rag is to arrange them roughly in order on a flat surface in a series of about twelve rows, figure 14.4(a). By the application of one small spot of adhesive one whole set can be glued together in a single operation, figure 14.4(b). Eventually whole rows will be assembled and these in turn can be brought together in a continuous line.

The multi-coloured 12 mm (½ in.) strip was wound with a

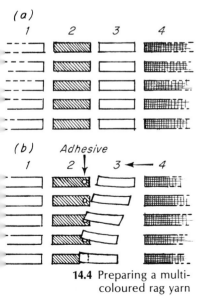

14.4 Preparing a multi-coloured rag yarn

130

14.5 Sample 3 Flat-woven rag

6 mm (¼ in.) wide plain strip onto one shuttle. This combination of two relatively narrow yarns means that the warp is effectively covered and a firm hardwearing surface established.

Should a pile rug be favoured or only small pieces be available, rags can be used to produce a knotted pile.

The pile rag, Sample 4, figure 14.6, was constructed in the same way as knotted Rya (chapter 7), on a cotton netting twine warp 16 single ends per mm (4 single ends per inch). The plain ground was woven in a medium weight cotton rag cut into 12 mm (½ in.) continuous strip. The pile consists of dress weight nylon/cotton/rayon/satin rag again cut into 12 mm (½ in.) wide strips. The pile is 50 mm (2 in.) long. There are eight picks between the rows of knots, while the individual knots consist of three rag ribbons in combinations of eight different colours.

Two other weaving methods already mentioned in previous sections are illustrated in figures 14.7 and 14.8.

In Sample 5, figure 14.7, wrapped loops are woven in coconut

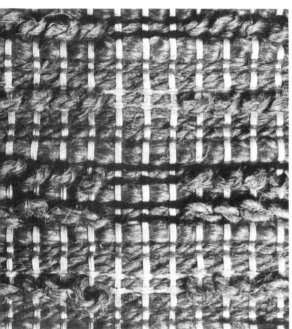

14.6 *Top* Sample 4 Rya rug

14.7 *Above left* Sample 5 Wrapped loops

14.8 *Above right* Sample 6 Weft chaining

fibre (coir) and dyed cottons between rows of unspun jute, and Sample 6, figure 14.8, shows a sample illustrating how weft chaining can be woven in a lightweight rope. This sample also contains dyed sisal and a fine cotton yarn to hold the heavier yarns in position.

Sample 7, figure 14.9, shows the effectivenes of the continuous

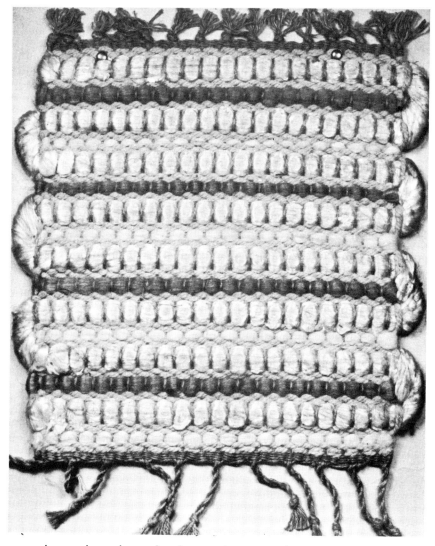

14.9 Sample 7 Continuous
selvedge loop

yarn looped at the selvedge to its next place in the shed. This
sample is an interesting combination of materials, being woven
with rayon tow, unspun flax, unspun delustred rayon, and cotton
across a linen warp.

Methods such as Khelim or tapestry weave can be used in the
context of matting where contrasting materials are woven into
shapes upon a plain ground. This type of design is always useful
when attempting to show off special materials. Here the positioning of the materials must be carefully considered to obtain the
maximum effect. Some materials if placed too closely all over the
design can lose their originality. On the other hand they may
benefit from being bunched closely together. When in doubt
always weave a sample first. Backgrounds for this type of matting
can be woven in either cotton or linen yarns, or a combination of
both. The weight of these yarns needs to be carefully considered.

Six to eight yarns mixed on the shuttle may be required to provide an adequate background weight.

The warp-faced weave Sample 8, figure 14.10, uses dyed linen, camel hair and cotton thread in a design which uses the concept of *thick* and *thin* warp yarns. In this example yarns are arranged in a symmetrical pattern and incorporate single strands as well as groups of up to fourteen threads. Spreading the warp was done on 24 ends per 100 mm reed (6 ends per inch) with many of the single threads sharing the same dents as the heavier yarns.

Linen is used throughout the weft; four single threads would be used together on one shuttle.

This sample was finished off by a method of cutting and gluing the warp ends which was possible owing to the firm, hard nature of the fabric. To achieve this edge, first remove the weaving carefully from the loom, (see page 136) and lay the rug *on its back* to decide the point at which the warp ends are to be cut. This point should first be marked with a fine chalk line across the weaving, and slightly *inside* the *woven* area of the rug so that the cut occurs between *two lines of woven weft*. Fabric adhesive should first be applied in a thin strip 12 mm (½ in.) wide up to the drawn line on the inside of the woven area, and allowed to dry. This will stop the weaving from falling apart during the cutting and gluing process. Using a sharp knife and a metal straight edge or scissors, cut along the chalk line, disposing of the waste.

14.11 Finishing off matting

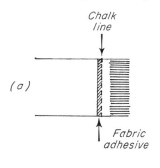

(a)

Chalk line

Fabric adhesive

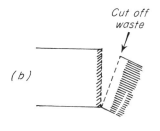

(b)

Cut off waste

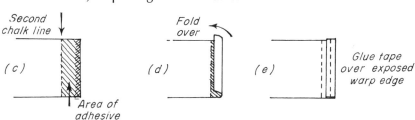

.Second chalk line

(c)

Area of adhesive

Fold over

(d)

(e)

Glue tape over exposed warp edge

134

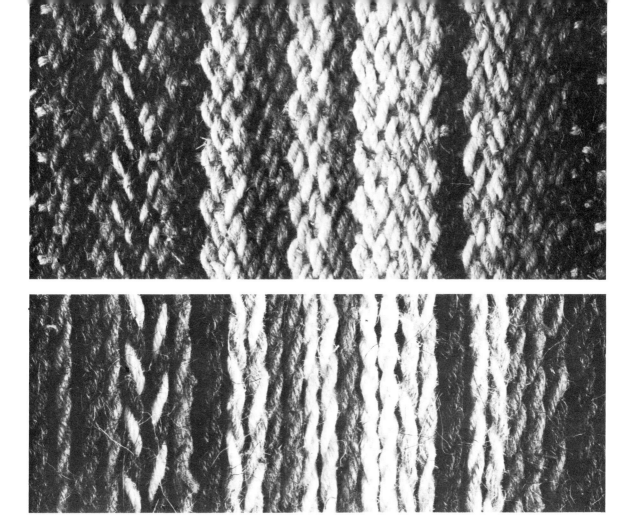

To protect the warp ends the edge should be folded back like a hem, and glued to a width of 25 mm (1 in.) on the underside of the mat. To do this a second line 50 mm (2 in.) should be drawn inside the first and adhesive carefully applied to this area. When the adhesive is at the correct drying stage fold back the edge to the second chalk line and press down hard making a turned edge of 25 mm (1 in.). This procedure should be applied to both ends of the weaving. To complete the process, 25 mm (1 in.) carpet binder should be ironed or glued over the exposed warp ends all of which will be on the underside of the matting. Figure 14.11 gives details in a series of simple diagrams.

Twisted yarns in contrasting tones are used throughout the warp-faced weave, figure 14.12. This sample illustrates the surface effect of these yarns when woven.

The arrangement of yarns prior to weaving is shown in figure 14.13, where the appearance strongly suggests Soumak or two-colour chain stitch. The warp is a combination of cotton, camel hair and linen thread, and the weft is natural linen only, consisting of four single threads wound onto one shuttle, and woven in plain weave.

14.12 *Top* Sample 9 Twisted thread warp weave

14.13 Arrangement of yarns prior to weaving

15 RUG FINISHES

When the final picks or *heading* of the rug have been completed it is essential to take a few precautions before cutting the rug from the warp. This is to ensure that the weft threads which are tightly compacted together remain in position and do not work loose. To do this it is necessary to weave an additional eight to ten picks of plain weave, in an unwanted length of yarn. These will correspond to the picks at the other end of the rug used for spreading out warp ends. *These extra rows must be retained until after the rug is positioned ready to receive its finished edges.* Next, slightly relax the high tension of the warp so that it remains fairly tight but not taut. This done, work from the centre of the warp and cut *two adjacent threads only*, about 225 mm (9 in.) long, knotting them, not too tightly, along the edge of the weaving. Proceed either side of centre, cutting and knotting at about 75 mm (3 in.) intervals alternately first one side then the other until the selvedge is reached. This done the whole warp can be cut to the same length. As already stated, the amount of warp yarn needed for finishing should be not less than 225 mm (9 in.) long. Less than this makes knotting or fringing more difficult.

The most practical position in which to work on the final fringe is to place the rug on a table with the edge to be worked along one side.

The rug must be held firmly in position. Heavy books or piles of magazines do well for this purpose and should be placed along the working edge.

When all is ready the extra picks woven to protect the *heading* can be carefully removed.

Do not remove these extra picks all at once. A strip of about 155 mm (6 in.) will give enough clear ends to work on at one time. Scissors will be needed to cut away the extra picks without disturbing the heading edge.

Overhand knotting

This is the most straightforward method of finishing off a rug, figure 15.1. Knots must be tied to lie hard against the woven edge for which some experience and skill is required.

One method of achieving this is to first tie the knot loosely, as close to the woven edge as possible. Divide the threads into two

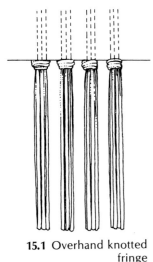

15.1 Overhand knotted fringe

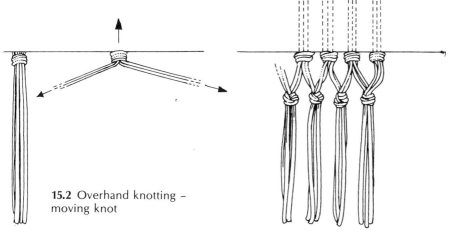

15.2 Overhand knotting –
moving knot

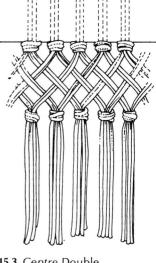

15.3 *Centre* Double
knotted fringe

15.4 *Above* Interlaced
knotted fringe

parts and pull apart, figure 15.2, forcing the knot to move towards
the rug. To achieve a really tight knot, each end should be pulled
individually. This procedure will ensure that however hard the
treatment, the knots are unlikely to work loose. Four single or two
double threads are recommended for each knot.

Plain knotting can be exploited in various ways to produce
decorative borders. After the first row of knots the ends are
divided into pairs and knotted again in another row to the adjacent pair at either side, figure 15.3. This process can be repeated
a second time if required and the warp sufficiently long.

Figure 15.4 shows a variation on this method. Here the ends are
interlaced before tying the second row of knots.

15.5 *Below* (a) to (e)
Plaited fringe

15.6 *Bottom* (a), (b) and (c)
Terminating plaited yarns
yarns with overhand knot

Plaited fringe

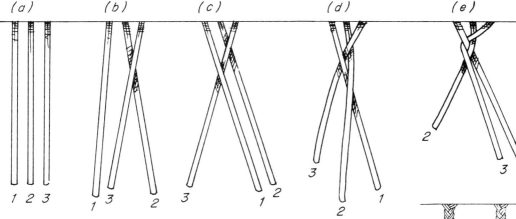

(a)   *(b)*   *(c)*   *(d)*   *(e)*

1 2 3   1 3   2   3   1 2   1 2   1   2   3 1
                                    3   3

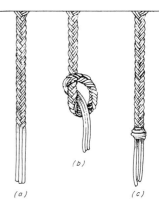

(b)

(a)   *(c)*

Plaiting is a quick and effective method of creating a simple rug
finish.

Using three ends of two strands is recommended. This makes a
delicate plait thin enough to finish with an overhand knot. After
crossing the strands two or three times pull each one tightly to
bring the plait close to the woven edge. Using the sequence in
figure 15.5, groups of yarns can be plaited to terminate in an overhand knot, figure 15.6(a), (b) and (c).

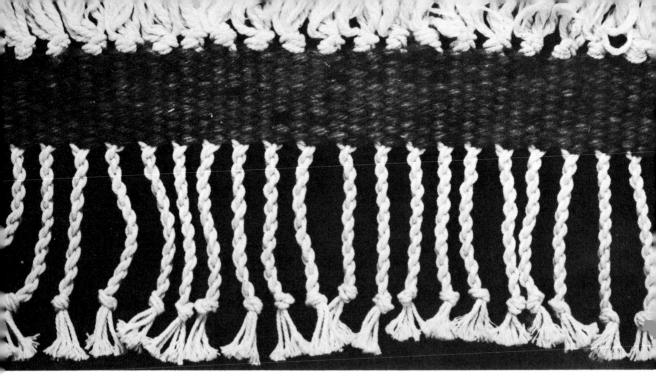

Plyed fringe Figure 15.7

Warp ends can be plyed to make the fringe resemble a series of 2-ply cords.

Select two pairs of adjacent threads and twist both pairs in the same direction, rolling them between thumbs and fingers, putting as much twist into the yarn as possible without the yarn bunching-up, over a length of approximately 65 mm (2½ in.). This done, bring both pairs together holding them firmly to stop any twist escaping and twist them both together in the opposite direction to the previous twist.

An overhand knot in the end will ensure that the yarn retains its twist. Figure 15.8 illustrates this technique.

15.8 (a), (b) and (c) Plyed fringe

(a)   *(b)*   *(c)*

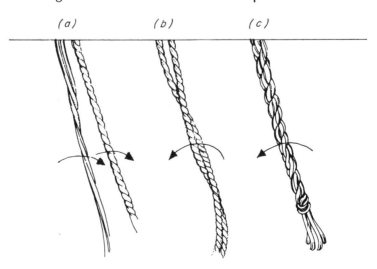

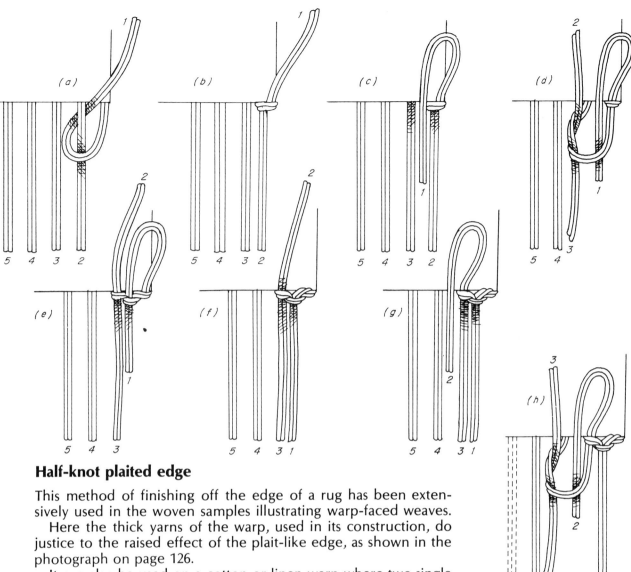

Half-knot plaited edge

This method of finishing off the edge of a rug has been extensively used in the woven samples illustrating warp-faced weaves.

Here the thick yarns of the warp, used in its construction, do justice to the raised effect of the plait-like edge, as shown in the photograph on page 126.

It can also be used on a cotton or linen warp where two single ends can create a neat plaited line. This edge, however, should be finally plyed or knotted to ensure that the edge is really secure. Figure 15.9 illustrates the procedure in a series of eight drawings.

Plaiting should start from the right. The right hand thread (1) passes over and round the left hand thread (2) in a half knot, figure 15.9(a). This should be tightened (not too tightly) so that it lies hard against the woven edge 15.9(b). Take the top thread (1) and bend it down in a loop to lie between the knot and the next thread (3) 15.9(c). Select the next thread (3) and repeat the half-knot 15.9(d) and (e). Then holding the two threads (2 and 3) firmly with the fingers of the left hand, pull thread (1) down to rest on the knot 15.9(f). Take thread (2), bend down half way in a loop as before, 15.9(g), and continue to repeat this sequence, 15.9(h), until the final thread is reached. This can be finished in a complete knot, the threads ending in the direction of the weaving being sewn into the woven edge with a needle.

15.9 (a) to (h) Half knot plaited edge

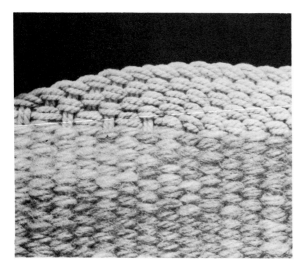

Woven edge Figure 15.10 *above*

There are various ways of creating a woven edge as a rug finish. Figure 15.10 illustrates one of the most straightforward of these.

Here the basic principle is to use the *warp* of the weaving as the *weft* thread, weaving it through at right angles along the side of the 'heading'.

Weaving starts at the bottom left hand corner working to the right and using a limited number .of picks only each time.

Weaving must be done with the right amount of slack so that when pushing-up, the weft covers the warp. With the heading held firmly in position the whole operation can be done with the fingers. As figure 15.11 shows, the weft is woven through ten ends after which it leaves the weaving along the finished edge. This is not a difficult procedure as the warp yarns can be lightly tensioned with the fingers of one hand while closing up the threads of the weft with the fingers of the other.

When the right hand corner of the woven edge is reached some weavers recommend terminating the weaving with a plait. In the woven sample shown in the photograph above, however, the end is finished to match the beginning, that is by gradually terminating the wedge-like shape.

This is done by sewing the ends back into the weaving, and to achieve this the following procedure is recommended:

Continue weaving in the warp with the fingers until the yarns reach the final warp selvedge thread, figure 15.12(a). *This weft thread is the one around which the remainder will turn before re-entering the weaving,* and is the *first* to be sewn into the heading. Sewing in must be done after *first circling the outside selvedge thread,* figure 15.12(b), entering the heading for approximately 25 mm (1 in.). The remaining warp threads will return into the weaving *following the same course through which they came out,* after first circling the weft thread already mentioned, figure 15.12(c).

1 2 3 4 5 6 7 8 9 10 11 12 13 14

15.11 Woven edge – diagram

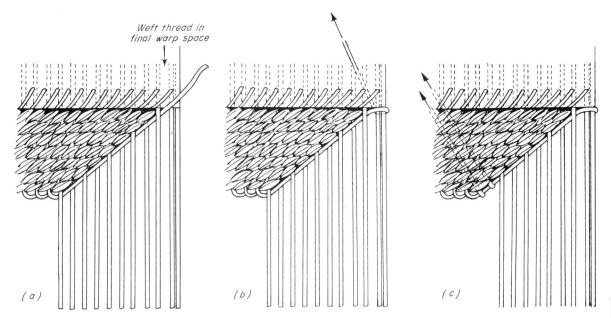

Weft thread in
final warp space

(a)   (b)   (c)

15.12 (a), (b), (c) and (d) Completing the woven edge

This operation is done with a large fine straight needle taking one thread at a time, each thread being sewn into the heading for about 25 mm (1 in.).

The final operation concerns the final right hand selvedge thread. This must turn back into its own warp space having made sure it is held fast by the weft thread that first circled it. Figure 15.14(d) describes this diagrammatically.

Cutting off all excess threads should be done after the edge is completed.

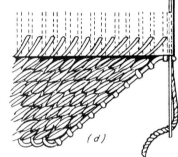

(d)

BIBLIOGRAPHY

Albers, Anni   *On Weaving* Wesleyan University Press, Middletown, Connecticut 1965

Beutlich, Tadek   *The Technique of Woven Tapestry* Batsford 1967 4th Impression 1979

Collingwood, Peter   *The Techniques of Rug Weaving* Faber 1968

Grierson, Ronald   *Woven Rugs* Dryad Press Leicester

Klares, Lewis and **Hutton**, Helen   *Rugweaving* Batsford 1962

Maile, Anne   *Tie and Dye Made Easy* Mills and Boon 1971

Reed, Stanley   *Oriental Rugs and Carpets* Weiderfeld and Nicholson 1965

Tattersall, C E C   *Notes on Carpet Knotting and Weaving* Victoria and Albert Museum 1961

Tovey, John   *The Technique of Weaving* Batsford 1965, new edition 1975

Tovey, John   *Weaves and Pattern Drafting* Batsford 1969, new edition 1978

SUPPLIERS

Europe

Anglia Fibres Ltd, Lady Lane Estate, Hadleigh, Ipswich, Suffolk
Plastic yarns

Craftsmans Mark Ltd, Trefnant, Denbigh, North Wales LL16 5UD
Welsh hand spun rug yarns in natural colours, 3-ply carpet yarn (white), flax, jute, rayon, sisal, linen yarns, three weights of loom cord

Dryad (Reeves) Ltd, Northgate, Leicester
Looms and weaving equipment and yarns. Catalogue on request

Fokeningen Hemslojden, Box 433, Boras, Sweden
Manufacturers of the Ulla Cyrus, a countermarch loom with overslung batten. Catalogue on request

A K Graupner, Corner House, 4 Valley Road, Bradford
Rug wool, looped mohair, looped worsted

Green Bros Ltd, Summerheath Road, Hailsham, E. Sussex
Coconut fibre (coir), jutes, ropes, etc

Harris Looms Ltd, Northgrove Road, Hawkhurst, Kent TN18 4AP
Manufacturers of upright rug looms and counter-march foot power looms, plus a range of weaving accessories. Catalogue on request

Helmi Vuorelma OY, Vesijarvenkatu 13, 15141 Lahti 14 Pl. 45, Finland
Wide range of dyed linen yarns. Bleached and unbleached linen tow. Range of Finnish woollen yarns

Frank Herring, 27 High West Street, Dorchester, Dorset

Looms and weaving equipment
J Hyslop Bathgate & Co, Victoria Works, Galashiels, Selkirkshire, Scotland
Looped and brushed mohair
H & J Jones, 58 Wood Street, Liverpool
Cotton yarns, hemp, jute ramie. Unspun hemp and jute available
Lervad (UK) Ltd, 18 Vernon Buildings, Westbourn Street, High Wycombe, Bucks
Looms of all types, plus a wide range of accessories. Catalogue on request
Loom Company Varpapuu, 76120, Pieksamaki, Finland, exported by Oy Varpa Looms Ltd, Osmontie 35, 46800 Myllykoski, Finland
Excellent looms of all types plus a wide range of accessories. Catalogue on request
John Maxwell, Folder Lane, Burgess Hill, Sussex
Hand-made looms to standard or individual specifications
Norsk Kunstvevgarn, Hombursand, pr Grimstad, Norway
Suppliers of Norwegian Spaelsau wool, 2-ply yarns in four different counts
Silken Strands, 33 Linksway, Gatley, Cheadle, Cheshire SK8 4LA
Supplies type of raffia yarn mid-way between a cellophane and plastic yarn
Somic Ltd, PO Box 8, Alliance Works, Preston PR1 5PS
Paper yarns
Southwick and Case, 38 Canning Place, Liverpool 1
Suppliers of hemp, jute and cotton yarns and cord
J & W Stuart Ltd, Esk Mills, Musselburgh, Scotland
Cotton matting twine. Samples on request
Textilose Ltd, Mosley Road, Trafford Park, Manchester M17 1PX
Paper yarns
Weavers' Shop, Royal Carpet Factory, Wilton, Nr Salisbury, Wilts

2-ply carpet wool, white and dyed colours, 'thrums' (odd ends)

USA

Looms and weaving equipment
Gilmore Looms, 1023 North Broadway Avenue, Stockton, California, CA 95205
Herald Looms, Bailey Manufacturing Company, 118 Lee Street, Ohio 44254
LeClerc Industries, PO Box 267, Champlain, New York
L W Macomber, 166 Essex Street, Saugus, Massachusetts

Yarns
Conlin Yarns, PO Box 11812, Philadelphia 19128
Fort Crailo Yarn Co, 2 Green Street, Rensselaer, New York, NY12144
Greentree Ranch Wools, 163 N Carter Lake Road, Loveland, Colorado 80537
Old Mill Yarn, PO Box 115, Eaton Rapids, Michigan 48827
The Yarn Depot, 545 Sutter Street, San Francisco, California 94102
The Yarnery, 1648 Grand Avenue, St Paul, Minnesota 55105

INDEX